Turn the Corner

Turn the Corner

Sex, Morality, Drinking, Money
Military/Colleges/World

Anita LaRaia

TATE PUBLISHING
AND ENTERPRISES, LLC

This book is designed to provide accurate and authoritative information with regard to the subject matter covered. This information is given with the understanding that neither the author nor Tate Publishing, LLC is engaged in rendering legal, professional advice. Since the details of your situation are fact dependent, you should additionally seek the services of a competent professional.

The opinions expressed by the author are not necessarily those of Tate Publishing, LLC.

Published by Tate Publishing & Enterprises, LLC
127 E. Trade Center Terrace | Mustang, Oklahoma 73064 USA
1.888.361.9473 | www.tatepublishing.com

Tate Publishing is committed to excellence in the publishing industry. The company reflects the philosophy established by the founders, based on Psalm 68:11,
"The Lord gave the word and great was the company of those who published it."

Book design copyright © 2016 by Tate Publishing, LLC. All rights reserved.
Cover design by Dante Rey Redido
Interior design by Shieldon Alcasid
Front Cover Photograph "Colonnade"— Copyright 2015 Lauren Kingsley Reed—All rights reserved.

Published in the United States of America

ISBN: 978-1-68301-195-8
Psychology / Human Sexuality
16.04.07

To every man and woman who has
served well in the U.S. Military.

ACKNOWLEDGMENTS

FOR ALL MY companions on the journey—family and friends who've given me a lifetime of love and understanding—I thank you with my whole heart. There's no sword in it because of you. I am healed. May you be also.

WHITE ROSES & PUSSY WILLOWS

Dad planted Pussy Willows at the front of our house that grew tall enough to reach our second-story bedrooms.

In the spring when their soft kitten-fur heads—as big as my young girl's thumb—burst into yellow bloom, their sweet, subtle scent made glorious the air from our open windows.

And in summer, as school ended, the entire right side of our house was an ecstatic celebration of a multitude of double-sized White Roses, whose unparalleled creamy pearl color a constant inspiration for our fresh complexions and souls.

I bury my face in those long-ago blooms in remembrance of the roaring-tiger Dad who planted them and made me fierce and fearless, and the saintly, singing farm girl Mom who told me, "*Turn the corner*...and you will move from the darkness into the light."

—Performed on YouTube.com:
Anita LaRaia's Video Poems-Six Poems Vol. 1

CONTENTS

White Roses & Pussy Willows..............................9

Introduction...13

1   Take Courage...15
2   Binge Drinking & Sexual Assault—U.S. Military...19
3   Binge Drinking & Sexual Assault—Colleges.........33
4   Math for World Peace................................39
5   Bravery and Control 47
     Nuns On The Bus—Teach The Teacher 52
     Drive 54
6   What Do Women Want 57
     Mirror Image & Something More.................60
7   Why Men Need Women 63
8   Good Luck Equals Right Thinking................71
9   Business 75
10   Violence, Women & the Military 79
11   A Woman President..................................85
     100 Million Votes...................................88
12   Wolf of Wall Street...................................91
13   Politics—My Party...................................97
     Holding Hands—Metaphysics 105

14 All Families Are Dysfunctional.............................. 107
    River Leaves & Muskrat Stillness.................... 114
15 My Husband—Jeweled Butterfly 117
    Jeweled Butterfly 119
16 Roaring-Tiger Dad 121
17 Sum Total 127
18 Writer, Fighter…Teacher 129
19 Shortcoming 133
20 Valedictorian 135
21 Karma Catch-Up 137
22 Something More.. 141
23 Diplomacy 143
24 Our World 145
25 Reality Check 147
26 Divine Mind 149
27 Parade Your Personality.. 153
28 Life of Pi.. 157
29 Domestic Violence.. 161
    Fifty Shades & Envisage Nothing.................... 165
30 Churches... 167
31 Last Poem 171
32 The Luck Factor.. 177
33 Work Is More Than a Job..................................... 181
    Sword Through the Heart................................ 183
34 Men Are from Venus, Women Are from Mars 185
35 Full Circle... 187

Epilogue 191

INTRODUCTION

RELATIONSHIPS—TO WORK COLLEAGUES, family, friends, neighbors, lovers, spouses, children, etc.—are the subject matter I've been studying for decades.

From my earliest years, I can remember looking deep into other people's souls. I was aware that in order to survive and succeed, I would have to understand the *why* behind their actions. What I discovered is that we often act at random without real reasons or purpose—and that causes both parties pain.

So much of life, particularly in families, is dysfunctional—the only difference is the degree of dysfunction. Therefore, we must all learn to get over the hurts and slights of childhood to become more self-actualized adults.

Love does not conquer all—though it goes a long way toward achieving victory. Another truth is that we are all human, and that means we are flawed, and on top of that, God gave us free will, and that's a lethal combination. What hurts us does indeed make us stronger.

And in fact, what we fail to acknowledge is that like an onion, we are adding layers to our personality that will stand the test of time and help us face and conquer our fears. This is the key to past, present, and future. This is how we make everything connect in perfect order so that we achieve maximum satisfaction in our personal and professional lives.

Nothing can stop you or even deflect your trajectory. If someone kicks your ball, then imagine it taking and staying on a new course of opportunities.

Roll your ball in that new direction, and you'll remain the master or mistress of your own destiny. Never give personal power over your life to anyone else but God.

By showing you how I've solved life's problems and with the inspiration of my ten free verse poems, I hereby give you the benefit of my experience (BOME) so that you can *Turn the Corner* and move from the shadows into the sunlight. But you must walk up to that corner and turn it. That is your obligation.

1

TAKE COURAGE

CAN WE MAKE the world we live in to our own specifications? Yes, it is not just possible but necessary for our well-being.

That is the fate we face as we breathe in life and breathe out any obstacles to our realizing the fullness of our gifts.

These are the gifts we were born to use for the greater good because our success as human beings is paramount to our purpose on earth—our mission.

All that I have lived and experienced before now was preparation for this task of completing this book and its message for you.

There is so much craziness, cruelty, and meanness around those who enable it. Don't enable other people's craziness—you have enough craziness of your own.

Be a force for good, bring light to the world where ignorance darkens, and climb that crystal stair to a heavenly existence that begins now and continues each day into forever.

Arriving in London, England—after touring Europe with housemates from Cornell University, Ithaca, NY, where I earned BA and Master's degrees in Social Psychology—it was a real game of survivor because I had no money, no job, no roof over my head, and no friends or contacts.

To say I was in mortal danger every moment is an understatement since I was a beautiful 24-year-old woman. I needed a bodyguard and income. Not wanting to alarm my parents or ask them for money—us early baby boomers didn't do that—I applied for various office jobs, slept on floors in hostels, and ate poorly.

Looking for encouragement from Heaven, I found myself in a blind alley and turned the corner to find an entire brick wall lit by a huge red neon sign: *Take Courage*. Mistaking it for a divine message telling me to persevere, I soon after got a job with a small American company, and after six years of registering with the police and because of my MA degree, I became a "working resident of Great Britain"—a desirable but hard-to-get designation stamped in my U.S. passport.

Little did I know that Take Courage was a beer sign, and it foretold the start of a decades-long career in the wine trade that began in London and continued in Atlanta, Georgia.

The London alcohol beverage experience working with nine wild men in a retail store in the red-light district off Piccadilly prepared me for a man's business, in which I was constantly surrounded by testosterone-fueled liquor salesmen and would be the only estrogen in the room.

Eventually, I turned the tables on the liquor salesmen and became their wine guru—hired by their bosses to train them in the thousands of wine labels their distributor houses sold. Yes, I am a wine expert, but more to the point, I know booze and all about binge drinking and its inevitable consequences.

2

BINGE DRINKING & SEXUAL ASSAULT—U.S. MILITARY

TAKING NOTES ON the national news every day from newspapers and TV and keeping a daily diary of my own activities since 1984, I was able to track several themes including the alcohol-related 88,000 annual death toll announced June 27, 2014, in conjunction with the CDC. That translated to the loss of 2.5 million years of life at a total cost to American society of $223 billion—or $1.90 per drink, a loss we can little afford. And underage drinking was a major cause of the 10,000 Americans killed and over 350,000 people injured in alcohol-related crashes in 2013 according to MADD—Mothers Against Drunk Driving.

Binge drinking is defined as the consumption of 5 or more alcohol drinks in a row for men or 4 drinks at one sitting for women. American moms were drinking whole bottles of Merlot, 40 percent of college students admitted binge drinking, and millions of teenage girls drink more hard liquor now than ever before. Yet of the one million alcoholics who go to rehab every year in the U.S., 90 percent will "fail rehab" and relapse, which means more costly future rehabs. The high price they pay is the risk of coma, death, and assault.

Women average 60 percent less of the detoxifying enzyme *alcohol dehydrogenase* in their stomach linings as men, and their levels fall to near zero sooner with heavy drinking, making them even more vulnerable. So it is physiologically impossible for women to drink as much as any man without putting their health at risk from liver damage, looking much older than their age, and placing themselves in real danger. I interviewed Dr. Harvey E. Finkel over the phone in 2005 about this fact and other research findings in his booklet "In Vino Sanitas?" published by the Society of Wine Educators.

A fallout from binge drinking is also sexual assault of young women—and surprisingly, young men too. The Department of Defense, or DoD, analysis of the estimated 26,000 sexual assaults in the U.S. Military in 2012 showed that 66 percent were attributed to the overconsumption of alcohol, i.e., binge drinking. By number, most sexual assaults in the Military that year were "men on men"—which must be very demoralizing for the good guys—but by percentage, since there are so few women in the Military, the rate was higher for "men on women" sexual assault. Getting more women recruits will require a protective infrastructure, which also protects the men. In the meantime, women must protect themselves by not bellying up to the bar to drink like the boys. That's not equality, that's foolishly ignoring the fact that you're in hostile territory where you are outgunned and outmanned.

The latest sexual assault report from the DoD, the 2014 Annual Report available on the Sexual Assault Prevention and Response Office website Sapro.mil, shows improvement in reporting—25 percent up from 11 percent in 2012. But more than half of the women reporting sexual assault perceived social retaliation for doing so. However, there was significant progress in decreasing the percent of women reporting unwanted sexual contact from 6.1 percent in 2012 to 4.3 percent in 2014. Unwanted sexual contact among Military men also trended downward from 1.2 percent in 2012 to 0.9 percent in 2014. With over 1.4 million active-duty U.S. Military personnel in the five service branches, the low percent of sexual assaults among the men is actually a number almost as big as that for the women since there are four times as many men in the Military as there are women, i.e., 80 to 93 percent men and approximately 7 to 20 percent women (depending on the branch of service).

I congratulate the U.S. Military for responding to Congress and President Barack Obama's strong mandates to change for the better with stricter procedures in the handling of these cases of sexual assault, including required notation in the personnel files of perpetrators, substantial enforcement of harsher penalties in the Uniform Code of Military Justice, and finally, the appointment of the first woman director of SAPRO on June 8, 2015: Two-Star Army Major General Camille M. Nichols.

Using every technology available in this digital age, they have created many effective tools for advocacy and prevention and to share resources. I also noted on the SAPRO Web site that the Coast Guard is to receive an award for implementation of innovative approaches to solving the problem of sexual assault, which the Military defines as rape, sexual assault, aggravated sexual assault, abusive sexual contact, nonconsensual sodomy, and attempts of these crimes.

But are the "root causes" being addressed by the Military? After a long in-person discussion with a retired woman Army Colonel who had worked for years in the Army's Human Resources Command, we arrived at the same conclusion: It might take twenty years to completely change the male-dominated culture of the Military through normal channels since it is so pervasive. But if the two root causes we agreed upon were effectively addressed, i.e., binge drinking and loss of moral compass, duty and discipline could be restored. She recommended I push to be heard on both topics through my writing and in what I call my "Shock & Awe" lectures—*shock* for the men who need to become better men and *awe* for the women who need a champion and to stiffen their own backbone.

Americans expect our Military to be moral leaders compared to our enemies' armies who rape and pillage as their spoils of war. But the Military must stop the sexist segregation of women service members even in their uniforms. I was told that there are no pants available as part of their new Army dress "blues"—the only option is a skirt that would make it difficult to run in an emergency. I saw a woman Admiral of the Coast Guard—very tall dignified older woman—forced to be the only officer enlisted in the room not wearing pants. Let the male "flag" officer show off their legs in panty hose and see how demeaning it is.

These recommendations would be especially timely as all branches of the U.S. Military have been ordered to recruit more women by January 1, 2016. I hadn't seen a single new recruitment advertisement geared toward attracting qualified women to the Armed Forces—except wonderful Air Force nurses in operating room scrubs—but no Air Force *flygirls* who can "redtail" as well as any of the flyboy pilots. Yet the October 25, 2015, CBS TV program *60 Minutes* included a woman U.S. Air Force bomber pilot flying missions from Qatar to destroy ISIS/ISIL (Islamic State) terrorist munitions depots in Iraq.

Everything changed for the better when two exceptionally brave and fit young women army officers passed the grueling 62-day Army Ranger course at Ft.

Benning, Georgia, on August 21, 2015. Within 3 weeks, the army had a new TV commercial "I Was a Soldier" on the Weather Channel—and on their website GoArmy. com/team, showing Army women in uniform as lawyers, pilots, and in combat fatigues kissing a baby daughter good-bye. Congratulations to these two new women Army Rangers—1st Lt. Shaye Haver and Capt. Kristen Griest, and Army Reserve Major Lisa Jaster who also graduated the Ranger course 62 days later in October—because their groundbreaking achievement caused the Army to announce two weeks later that the Ranger School was now open to all qualified female soldiers.

So why not promote the real glamour jobs for women in the U.S. Military? I wrote, and hereby copyright, a funny commercial that would entice qualified American women to join the Military: "You don't have to be a Tom to be a *top gun* U.S. Navy pilot, you can be a Katie!" Everyone got the humor. So what if you get a huge response for what are very few such positions? Choose the cream of the crop and find a genuine place for them.

Same for the Military academies who train Navy, Marine, Army, Air Force Officers, and ROTC programs at colleges—it's already too late to recruit more women for this class year but maybe you can get qualified women to apply for next year. The Military needs a lot more women officers to lead and supervise new women recruits. Top brass know they need more women in the Military to be "battle ready" because there simply aren't enough qualified men since the draft ended in 1973. Right now, there aren't enough women in the Military to watch their own backs. Until that critical number is reached, they will not be safe without self-defense initiatives, and I have several ideas for those.

I used to call on every Military installation—and there were a lot more of them then—in Georgia when I worked for a large wine import company, and I saw firsthand what could be done to help prevent alcohol abuse and consequent sexual assault. Military officers I spoke with recently worried that the good guys would be penalized unfairly if limits were placed on alcohol purchases on base—and that anyway, soldiers and sailors are clever enough to get around any restrictions.

Maybe so, but we're talking potential security breaches from both Military and civilian personnel, particularly on large Army bases where gangs of enlisted men have been arrested by the FBI for sex trafficking, prostitution, and drug running on base—the Atlanta Journal-Constitution, a Pulitzer Prize–winning newspaper, ran this story which took place at Ft. Stewart near Savannah, Georgia. The year before, there had also been an execution-style murder of a former Army enlisted man and his fiancé there. Questions: Why didn't the MPs (military police) investigate these crimes when committed? Why would criminals want to join the Army and be subject to both Military justice and civilian laws? (Because these large army bases must be great "cover" for their nefarious enterprises). And why didn't the Army's own CID (criminal investigative division) investigate this conspiracy?

A retired Army Officer who had been stationed at Ft. Stewart told me, "Recruitment is the problem." Criminals must be weeded out during Recruitment before they are sworn into the Military and cause years of havoc. As I understand it, psychological profiles are kept of all active-duty Military, but I could not find any psychological testing done during Recruitment—along with the physical and written exams and random drug testing—in the book titled *Joining the United States Army: A Handbook* by Snow Wildsmith. For specific requirements for joining each branch of service, go to their individual website, or TodaysMilitary.com—though that website had no photos of women in uniform, none at all.

It's not that the Military doesn't do psychological studies. I was told by a retired Army Colonel who is an MD/psychiatrist still doing PTSD counseling for the VA—not just from the battlefield but also for both male and female survivors of sexual assault—that Walter Reed Hospital has an Institute of Military Psychiatry and that the Army Research Institute and Surgeon General's Offices conduct psychiatric research. All three have studied Military women but may not be asking the right questions to get the answers needed to really improve their status.

For example, the Army psychiatrist told me one problem is that the men and women in the barracks are no longer sleeping in open bays but in dorm-like apartments, leaving the women more vulnerable to hidden sexual assault. Alcohol fuels sexual assaults, even more so among much less mature, underage, i.e. teenage, enlisted recruits on base or at Military academies where hazing of the women is as frequent as it was decades ago. He went on to say that young people today mirror our larger society where immoral behavior is rampant among adults.

A former active duty Marine Colonel told me his experience indicated that today's enlisted recruits need "character development" and "respect-for-others" instruction in boot camp because they have not received this and other life lessons from their parents.

If you are already an American Military veteran, I hope you have discovered MilitaryOneClick.com, which is a very valuable Web resource to every installation in the U.S. and to the most popular blogs written by Military spouses and veterans of all branches of service, including Jenny Pilcher's well-written Navy spouse blog. The Marine blog USMC written by a male marine veteran, for example, has one million annual visitors.

Also, you can buy and drink *Service Compass Rose* beer from veteran-owned and veteran-operated Service Brewing Co. located in Savannah, Georgia—Marine, SerivceBrewing.com. Compass Rose beer is an India pale

ale, or IPA, with citrus flavors, and the profits support veterans' causes. Female veterans receive practical help so they don't become homeless from the nonprofit charity FinalSaluteInc.org.

And the USO—website USO.org—celebrates its 75th anniversary with new programs for our troops which you can support, such as Phone Home which provides phone cards and the technology to stay connected to loved ones back home.

By the way, Congress lifted the ban on Military women in combat in January 2013. And by January 1, 2016, commanders in each of the 5 branches of service—Army, Navy, Marines, Air Force, and Coast Guard—must open all roles to women or justify why a certain job should remain men only. *People* magazine, May 4, 2015, had an article "Real-Life GI Janes" about women soldiers who quietly serve, risk their lives and have died alongside Special Forces in Afghanistan under enemy fire. Women soldiers have already served in both Iraq and Afghanistan war zones, doing amazing stuff according to one Army General.

However, an Associated Press news article dated September 19, 2015, with the headline "Marines seek to keep women out of combat. Exclusion in conflict with stance from other services" announced that new chairman of the Joint Chiefs—4-Star General Joseph Dunford, who was commandant of the Marine Corps—is recommending that women be excluded from certain frontline combat jobs, mainly infantry, tanks, some artillery jobs, and reconnaissance positions. General Dunford submitted this to Secretary of the Navy (and Marines) Ray Mabus, who had already made it clear that women in the Navy or Marine Corps should be allowed to compete for combat jobs.

This puts General Dunford at odds with the Army, Navy, Air Force, and U.S. Special Operations Command—including Navy SEALS—who have said such an exclusion of women isn't warranted. Secretary of Defense Ashton Carter will review the Marine plan. Though it may be years before women even try to enter these fields, the point to my mind is that any active-duty woman Marine is entitled to enter combat training by the mere fact that she's already a Marine!

Having been married to a former active duty Marine for 33 years, I can tell you any woman who makes it has to be tough.

An Associated Press article dated January 9, 2016 details objections to Marine women in combat by two other USMC Generals--John Kelly and current Marine Commandant Robert Neller. They worry standards will have to be lowered for women, and they want to keep their basic training as it is now, separate from men. The Marines are the only ones who do this, and Secretary Mabus wants integration. Though the Marines admit sexual harassment or assault may be a result. USMC Commandant General Neller had the good sense since then to actually ask active duty Marine women what they thought. He discovered many are already working out with weights in the gym to "bulk up" for strenuous combat training. They're obviously not waiting to be told--they're taking full advantage of the potential opportunity. Good for them! Whether young women, like young men at age 18, will need to register for the draft is being discussed.

On December 3, 2015, Secretary of Defense Ash Carter announced that the Pentagon will open all combat jobs to Military women in all branches of service with no exceptions by early 2016. This groundbreaking decision overturns a 1994 Pentagon rule that restricted women from combat roles, though 300,000 women served in combat in Iraq and Afghanistan war zones over the last 14 years, and 6,000 (2%) of them lost their lives.

The only request for exemption came from the Marine Corps which has a 93% male (7% female, i.e. only 14,201 women) force dominated by infantry and a culture that segregates recruits by gender for basic training. Secretary Carter said all of the U.S. Military should operate under common standards. The *New York Times* article which broke this story said the Army was 14% women—twice that of the Marines—the Navy 17% and Air Force 19% for a total of 203,836 active duty Military women in 2013. This change was hailed by all Military women because without combat experience, they were unfairly held back from promotions. About 220,000 such positions are now a possibility for them as they are for men.

A member of the Georgia Vietnam Veterans Alliance, Norm Hapke, Jr., wrote a comprehensive article about women in combat for their January 2016 newsletter including their experiences in Canada & Israel, the 5 million women who fought worldwide in WWII and the fact that women may not do well in infantry jobs but have excelled as fighter pilots, aboard warships, base security and dealing with IEDs in convoy.

Yes, some combat positions may not be do-able for women, but that's implementation of the policy, and that will be worked out. No one will put Military women in combat jobs such as artillery if that will cause them to fail or injure themselves. I ask General Dunford and the Marines to restate their objection because right now it appears as if the Marine Corps is not supporting their own women Marines compared to Army, Navy, and Air Force women. Yet women Marines are just as much the "few and the proud" as Marine men.

Finally, November 11 Veterans Day—11/11/2015—is the start of a campaign by GreenLightAVet.com to get Americans to change one visible porch or office light to green and keep it glowing green every day as a symbol of support and appreciation for veterans.

As for one of the best new recruitment advertisements, I saw a great one with a woman lead for GoCoastGuard. com along with the trailer for the new movie "The Finest Hours" about the greatest U.S. Coast Guard rescue ever.

What men in the Military and everywhere else refuse to acknowledge is that: "If the women are happy, everyone is happy. And if the women are not, no one is."

3

BINGE DRINKING & SEXUAL ASSAULT—COLLEGES

PARENTS MUST ALSO stop the tsunami of alcohol abuse, and that includes lobbying colleges they pay good money to in tuition to throw fraternities off campus if they engage in sexual assault of coeds. This has already happened on several college campuses. My own alma mater, Cornell University, just reported February 7, 2016 the arrest of a Fraternity guy for the sexual assault and attempted rape of a coed which prompted the woman President of Cornell--Elizabeth Garrett--to suspend that Fraternity from the campus. And, the president of Dartmouth outlawed all hard liquor on campus to protect his coeds from high-proof fraternity drinks that cause immediate intoxication of naive 18-year–old freshmen girls.

In the December 4, 2014, *Rolling Stone* magazine article about sexual assault and rape of freshmen coeds, there was reference to a recent social psychological study that showed fraternity members were three times more likely to commit sexual assault than other male students at the same universities. No matter that the reporter who wrote the *Rolling Stone* article had to retract it and was unjustly reviled for not interviewing the accused gang-raping fraternity guys. That was just the "good old boy network" of fraternity alumni, led by the male bastion of the *Wall Street Journal*, blowing smoke to obfuscate the facts to protect their own self-image. The old saying "Boys will be boys" was never a valid excuse for rape.

Neither the attorneys nor the parents of these accused fraternity rapists would have ever allowed them to go on the record, or be quoted, by any national publication. It would be almost a tacit admission of guilt to show knowledge of the crime in a public forum. And yes, the university in question did have a filed report of the rape with the offenders' names, but no action had been taken against them.

The Justice Department will be investigating 89+ universities for their failure to protect coeds or prosecute those guilty of the crimes under Civil Rights Law and Title IX, which gives all women and girls equal access to educational activities, including sports, and requires all schools to report, counsel, investigate, take action against, and prevent the abuse of women and girls.

CNN aired the disturbing documentary *The Hunting Ground* on November 22, 2015, which told the story of the rape and sexual assault of college girls at dozens of colleges and universities from Berkeley to Notre Dame. Clinical psychologist David Lisak was quoted throughout the film because of his extensive research of this topic, and said colleges protect their "brand" by not reporting, investigating, or prosecuting sexual assaults as required by Federal law. One in 4 college girls in the U.S. are raped or sexually assaulted yet they result in zero expulsions at most of these schools.

Alcohol is used as a weapon to render these underage coeds vulnerable and the number of potential victims is endless, which is why colleges have always been a "hunting ground" for male predators who are mostly repeat offenders. Research studies show that only 8% of men will ever rape or sexually assault a woman or women, but that can be a very large number considering how many college or Military men there are.

At Hollywood's televised 88th Academy Awards, February 28, 2016, Vice-President Joe Biden made a special appearance to talk about men & women survivors of sexual assault on college campuses and to promote the website ItsOnUs.org Then Lady Gaga sang the Oscar-nominated song she wrote for the film The Hunting Ground called "Until It Happens To You" surrounded by a group of male & female college student survivors of sexual assault. It was very moving. That's why I cheered during the documentary when two young women rape survivors—whose rapists were never prosecuted—at the University of North Carolina, Chapel Hill fought back and filed a complaint with the Department of Education under Title IX and won a full hearing. This is what finally got the Justice Department involved.

According to a new 2015 report from the Bureau of Justice Statistics, 88 percent of rapes and sexual assaults of female college students go unreported, compared to 67 percent in the general population. Why? Because most college coed sexual assaults involve heavy drinking—or being drugged—which impairs the woman student's ability to bear witness or provide evidence. This has been going on for decades, even though the U.S. Congress passed the Violence Against Women Act in 1994 and voted to reauthorize the landmark law in 2013.

Proof that this is still very much a problem today was brought home to me in January 2016 when CBS Evening News reported that a young woman had been in a coma from binge drinking, and the 18 year old daughter of a friend had been rushed to the hospital with alcohol poisoning outside the university fraternity house where she had been attending her first ever college party. Watch out girls, fraternity guys are still putting 150 proof grain alcohol in that sweet punch they serve innocent first-year coeds.

As for the sexual abuse of boys at any school or college, all teachers are obliged to report such abuse to the police. The abusers are pedophiles and must face the full punishment of the law. Men in my family actually argued against me when I said famous Coach Joe Paterno of Penn State would suffer the ignominy of having his statue taken down from its pedestal on campus for failing to report the sexual molestation of young boys by one of his assistant coaches in the showers of his own football building. I said at the time he disgraced his Italian Catholic background and his sacred trust as a teacher.

Fame versus infamy—so many men, such as Oscar Pistorius, Jared Fogle (former Subway spokesperson who pleaded guilty to sex crimes), and Daniel Holtzclaw (former Oklahoma City police officer) who was sentenced to 263 years in prison for rape and sexual assault of women while on duty, fail to realize that their celebrity status or uniform does not mean they are above the law.

Sex crimes are being taken very, very seriously now in the U.S. The fact that Bill Cosby is facing criminal charges for sexual assault years later means there is zero tolerance. All guys need to think twice before even attempting to force a girl or woman to have sex.

By the way, Oscar Pistorius has now been charged with murder—after spending just 1 year in jail on a lesser charge—in the death of his girlfriend, and will now face a possible 15-year prison sentence when he is resentenced next year in South Africa.

And that goes double for priests in the Catholic Church and Military Sergeants who prey on very young and vulnerable recruits—both men and women. The latter was confirmed to me by that retired Army Colonel Psychiatrist. I was a teacher for 33 years, and I personally find it unforgivable that evildoers in these two groups of men abuse their positions as mentors. Again, these despicable co-workers must be very demoralizing for the dedicated priests and sergeants who try always to do what is right.

4

MATH FOR WORLD PEACE

IN MATH OR computer science, algorithms are self-contained step-by-step sets of operations for calculations, data processing, and automated reasoning. Algorithms were used by Alan Turing—subject of a recent Hollywood movie—when he developed his code-breaking Turing machines in the UK during WWII.

Dr. Bruce Bueno de Mesquita, professor at New York University and a senior fellow at Stanford, has used algorithms to become a modern-day Nostradamus among political and foreign policy forecasters. He has been able to predict the outcomes of war, nuclear proliferation, and political campaigns based on the past.

What he discovered is that most world leaders have been self-serving and dictatorial, acting in their own interests and not in the interests of their people. There may be no way to negotiate with such leaders, or as a prime example, to ever win a war in the Middle East. I also refer you to retired Marine Four-Star General Tony Zinni's book *Before the First Shots Are Fired* about war in the Middle East based on 900 years of that region's history and our own American Military history. General Zinni was former Commander in Chief of CentCom.

My own observations about the Middle East are based on both science and the Bible, which contrary to the misinterpretation of many, are not at odds. The story of Abraham is that for 4,000 years he has been considered the ancestor of both Jews and Muslims. God miraculously granted Abraham two sons—the first, Ishmael, is called the father of the Arab Nations because his 12 sons led the 12 warrior tribes of the Middle East. Abraham's second son, Isaac, is called a patriarch of the Jewish Nation because his son Jacob's 12 sons led the 12 tribes of Israel.

Rick Steves's recent PBS travel segment took viewers inside the tomb of Abraham in Hebron in the West Bank and showed both Palestinian Muslims and Jews worshipping there—separated by a wall. And a TV documentary on the Holy Land hosted by Christiane Amanpour on CNN featured scientists who had used DNA to prove that both Jews and Muslims of the region share the same genetic heritage. They fight brother against brother—they are even mistaken for each other during these skirmishes according to a recent Associated Press article.

Dr. Bueno de Mesquita begs U.S. leaders to use high-tech tools to avoid bad decisions that could lead to domestic catastrophe or a possible world war, as do I. When I am asked what my personal ambition is, I reply, "World peace." That must really be everyone's goal—especially in the Military.

The only time I see our soldiers with smiles on their faces is when they bring aid and comfort to the survivors of natural disasters. When hurricanes Katrina and Rita hit New Orleans and the Gulf Coast of the U.S. in 2005, it was Army 3-Star Lieutenant General Russel Honoré who saved the day. For his incredibly impressive credentials, go to GeneralHonore.com. He is now retired after 37 years of Military service, has a new book out titled *Leadership in the New Normal*, and is a CNN disaster preparedness coordinator. Also, our troops were heroes during Superstorm Sandy and now battle wildfires for us in the West. Protecting, defending, aiding, and comforting our citizens must always be our Military's first priority.

Putting my "think tank" brain to work to solve some of the world's most intractable problems, I have come up with potential diplomatic solutions:

- To really change the culture of the Middle East, we need to enhance the status of their women. National Geographic magazine's December 2015 issue with the Virgin Mary on the cover explained that the Mother of Jesus is the only woman with her own "sura" or chapter in the Koran and that Muslims revere her. The Holy Mother's many miracles and apparitions are detailed in this issue devoted to "the most powerful woman in the world." Muslims believe Jesus was the second most important prophet after Muhammad. And speaking of Muhammad, it was his literate wife whom he adored who codified his visions and revelations into the tenets of Islam. Her tomb is among the most impressive of Islamic holy sites. It may surprise Americans to learn that women in Saudi Arabia were only granted the right to vote in 2015.

- How can Muslim extremists believe virgins will be waiting for them in Heaven when they defile every woman and girl that crosses their path on earth? Allah is not pleased. It may seem glamorous to the delusional youths Islamic terrorists recruit to be given a stolen "bride," i.e., kidnapped schoolgirls, like the 219 taken by the Nigerian terrorist group Boko Haram (who remain missing as I write this). But it's really all about the money for their leaders— they are worse than Somali pirates. Someone please follow the money and stop it from reaching them. Looks like I was correct about this because after the horrible Paris massacre, French war planes began bombing ISIS-controlled oil fields in Syria and Iraq because ISIS is using these oil fields to get $1 million a day on the black market to fund their terrorism.

- I will not leave helpless women and girls to their total lack of mercy or humanity. And neither will President Barak Obama and First Lady Michelle Obama who launched Let Girls Learn in 2015 to encourage other countries to provide education for the 62 million girls worldwide who do not attend school. They announced a U.S. pledge of $70 million to help educate 200,000 girls in Pakistan. Culture is no excuse for abuse under U.S. law, and that includes genital mutilation and honor killings.

- The key to getting Bashar al-Assad out of Syria may be his British-born wife. Both his mother and sister have gone into exile in United Arab Emirates. If his wife were to join them, Bashar al-Assad could save face by telling the world that he and his three young sons love and miss her and that he and they will join her there. Syria is nothing but rubble after four years of civil war, but if Assad goes, maybe the millions of homeless Syrian refugees would return to their home country. Assad already faces war crimes charges by the world tribunal, and he would be torn apart by his own people like Gaddafi was in Libya if he ever walked out of his palace prison. Perhaps if we got every eye doctor in the U.S.— Assad is a London-trained eye doctor—to write and ask him to open his eyes, he might see reason.

- Putin is the wild card in Syria now that he has Russian planes bombing the country, (though not necessarily against ISIS but rather rebel forces opposing Assad), from an airfield he built there. But even he would not be immune to the loss of national pride if Americans would simply stop buying Russian vodka. We have plenty of choices for vodka martinis—Ketel One from Holland, Grey Goose from France, Absolut from Sweden, American-made Smirnoff, etc. Bars and liquor stores could simply refuse to reorder Russian Stolichnaya Vodka until Putin is out of Syria and the Ukraine. Wait! Let's not boycott Russian vodka for now because our enemy Putin became our friend when ISIS became his enemy too after they bombed a Russian Metrojet out of the sky just before the Paris massacre. Then Turkey shot down one of Putin's Syria-based warplanes which Putin said was a "stab in the back". Having a mutual enemy changes everything. By the way, ISIS members are Sunni Muslim, and they have killed more Shiite Muslims than Westerners. Again, it's brother against brother, even brothers of a different sect of Islam. Unfortunately, lots of women and children are killed in the crossfire.

- Finally, there's Kim Jong-un of North Korea. I've always wondered why his country is a wasteland that cannot grow enough food to feed his starving people. Perhaps a delegation of agricultural scientists could make thousands of small farms, even fish (aquaculture) farms, bumper-crop productive. But the world must be very careful to control sale of the harvests, or North Korean leaders will try to profit by selling them to other countries for cash. North Korea's leader(s) would rather spend what little their economy produces on missiles which they are defiantly testing. Are these threatening actions meant to get us to remove economic sanctions, or don't they care? Maybe dangling this agricultural help will induce them to make concessions.

5

BRAVERY AND CONTROL

BRAVERY AND CONTROL are foremost in my mind as I write this book—bravery because it is fear that holds us back at every juncture when a decision must be made, and control because without it, bravery can get us in deep trouble. As Cody Lundin, former barefoot survivalist on the *Dual Survivor* TV show, used to say, "Do dumb-ass things—get dumb-ass consequences."

I was "too brave for my own good" when I insisted on staying in London without any planning ahead or preparation. The protection I needed came from within as I sat in the dark during rolling blackouts of power outages at that time in England before they were able to tap into North Sea oil reserves.

No one to blame but myself. I had nowhere to look but within. I had to determine my soul's worth and decide whether I had foolishly thrown myself into the crucible that would burn through extraneous meaning and forge steel as both my mother and grandfather had done working in a steel mill for the U.S. WWII war effort. The revelations that came to me were that I was stubborn to a fault and so independent as to be a danger to myself. But it is exactly these traits that got me to the top of my high school class and six years at Cornell and the strength to start all over again in Atlanta after London.

London was the hardest thing I had ever done in my life, but it made me who I am today: an artist with words—on paper and speaking to an audience—and a teacher of compassion, tolerance, and practical wisdom. No regrets, because the experience turned my innate talents into skills that brought me income and legendary status among my graduates for years in Atlanta.

I will never forget the night we all watched Nik Wallenda walk a tightrope across the Grand Canyon. Even Rev. Joel Osteen said on camera that he couldn't watch at one point. It was riveting, and I couldn't take my eyes off the accomplishment. The same feeling of exhilaration I had when I watched Nik, grandson of the famous tightrope walker Karl Wallenda, walk across Niagara Falls. Talk about an adrenaline rush! Courage, prayer, and nerves as steely as the wire he walked on got him across and can get you anywhere.

As examples of the sacred and sexy in my life, I refer you to two more of my free verse poems (meaning they don't have to rhyme or be a certain meter—Walt Whitman wrote free verse poems): "Nuns on the Bus—Teach the Teacher" and "Drive." "Drive" is my funny double-entendre car-talk tribute to American men. Men need to control their masculinity, while women need to control access to their bodies and hearts so that we put self-love first in order to love another deeply but properly. Years ago, I was a follower of the self-love guru Erich Fromm who had this as his mantra.

And I wrote my "Nuns" poem because I heard best-selling author Brad Meltzer ask us all to acknowledge our best teachers at a book signing for his riveting *History Decoded: The 10 Greatest Conspiracies of All Time*. This is fascinating stuff, each chapter—such as what happened to Lincoln's assassin John Wilkes Booth—contains a pocket with copies of real documents as evidence. And I am happy to report that Cardinal Sean O'Malley of Boston—on CBS TV program *60 Minutes*, September 6, 2015—called the crackdown on American nuns by the Catholic Church a "disaster," and that the nuns no longer had to be supervised by the three bishops appointed by the Commission on Church Doctrine for focusing too much on social justice. So God answered the prayer in the last line of my poem.

But Cardinal O'Malley—the Pope's right-hand man in charge of overcoming the Catholic Church's scandal of child-molesting priests—fell all over himself trying to explain why women, including nuns, are not allowed to even study for the priesthood when U.S. seminaries are nearly empty. The cardinal said it was because Jesus had established the Church to have men only in the hierarchy. I went to Catholic school and defy him to show proof of that! I bet the Holy Mother Mary that all priests pray to every day must be very displeased. As displeased as she must have been when President Putin of Russia kept the Pope waiting during his Vatican visit while he bent down and kissed a golden icon painting of the Madonna. And yet Putin was quoted as saying, "All women are weak—and maybe that's a good thing." Wrong—it is never a good thing, and it is not true.

Holy Father, Pope Francis, why not let U.S. seminaries, which are colleges that train priests, accept qualified American Catholic women, including nuns? Yes, it will take years to train them as priests—but at least they will be in the pipeline. And they can do on-the-job training by assisting parish priests with certain duties and keep a watchful eye to make sure there are fewer opportunities for sin.

Please refer to Chapter 30, "Churches," for review of new movie *Spotlight* about the Boston Globe first breaking the story of pedophile priests in the U.S.

My poems are about love in its many forms—parental love, romantic love, marital love, love of nature, etc. And all of them are on less than a page when typed in 14 pt. A photojournalist friend in England—one of the nine men I worked with at that wine and liquor store in London—called my poems descriptive writing of the highest order and compared them to Marcel Proust's seven-volume memoir *A La Recherché du Temps Perdu*. I had to look that one up in Wikipedia. Years of writing discipline enables me to put it concisely and precisely.

You can see me perform all ten of my poems on YouTube.com—search "Anita LaRaia's Video Poems"; then click on *3 Valentine's Day Poems*, which features all aspects of my personality in 6 minutes; then click on *Six Poems Vol 1* (9 minutes); and finally view *Sword Thru the Heart*. Please write your comments underneath and become a free subscriber. You'll see a graduate student in women's studies wrote that I have exactly captured the dynamics between men and women. She wanted me to be their muse and Joan of Arc. We all know Joan of Arc was burned at the stake, but as a Military General, she won every battle for God and the French king, became a saint, and is still an icon of feminine strength 584 years later.

NUNS ON THE BUS—TEACH THE TEACHER

To this day, we don't know how Dad afforded it, but he sent us to Catholic middle school taught by the Sisters of St. Joseph.

Those convent nuns were angels in full black habits with starched-white wimples and rosary and cross waist belts. Dedication and discipline were their holy orders, which became the basis for our higher learning.

It was Sister Rose Gertrude who forced me to become a writer. In 8th grade, my assignment was to write a play for the class and to give every child a part that fit their personality. I was petrified of disappointing her faith in me.

Talent nurtured by these otherworldly nuns would lead to a worldly career. From my valedictory speech on moral complacency at age 17 to the scholarships that sent me to Cornell and a Master's degree in social psychology, these truly chaste brides of Christ planted the seed of my future income from hundreds of published wine articles and thousands of my own adult students.

Unblemished in spirit, fiery gurus burning with divine love for us—the only children they would ever have—these nuns were strong womanly role models that made me feel the equal of anyone. How can men in the church hierarchy possibly find fault with American "Nuns on the Bus"? Dressed in street clothes, these nuns none-the-less help the poor and heal the sick.

A lifetime of sacrifice is not disobedience. As you read this, I ask you, did the nuns do right by me? Please Holy Father, Pope Francis, do right by them.

DRIVE

Working my way around a map of the world as a beautiful young woman on her own in London, I was often asked, "Who were the best lovers?" American men, I'd say, they're the most experienced.

Much of their experience was acquired as testosterone-fueled teenagers in the backseat of cars. Off to a jackrabbit start, accelerating and careening around corners, they tore up the track with internal combustion and rocketing pistons.

What a thrill ride! Four-on-the-floor, blew the doors off, heart-racing climb to the finish line—these encounters were built for speed, and sadly there was no slowing for curves when the driver was high.

The first time I saw a brand-new Maserati sterling silver work of art gleaming in the Silicon Valley sun, I got it. Cars are chick magnets designed to drive girls wild. But 007 "Nobody does it better" James Bond didn't need the Aston Martin. He wooed women with smoldering looks, soft touches, and sensual kisses.

Watching very handsome American actor Ryan Gosling in the 2011 movie *Drive* expertly handle the stick shift of his bomber getaway car, I realized how much I admired a man who was in control of his stick. Guys, if you really want to avoid treacherous tailspins in life, always keep control of your stick.

And the secret to having a happy love life is to choose a woman who's in control of her stick. Then you'll both avoid road blocks, U-turns, stop signs, or crashes that total your wheels and you won't have to put on the brakes as you cruise to ecstasy. Rev your engines—*vroom, vroom*!

6

WHAT DO WOMEN WANT

I MAKE NO apology for being a feminist because being born an American woman who achieved years of higher education and was still treated like a second-class citizen in the land of the free and the brave has been hard to accept. Yes, I get it, men—why should you give up any privilege as first-class citizens to women who do virtually everything for you without demanding quid pro quo? Truth is our plumbing is not only different from men, it's painful plumbing—and most men on earth would never voluntarily change places with a woman or take on the burden of bearing children and, in addition, accept lower societal and financial status.

Also, being born in a hardworking household of modest means has powered my liberal mind-set and desire to be a positive role model for all women. Especially those who made the mistake of sacrificing themselves for a love that wasn't true—some even went to prison for it, being stupid enough to do what some con man told them to do. 94 percent of U.S. prisoners are men, only 6 percent women—although women make up more than half of the U.S. population. Yes, there are bad women, even criminals and evildoers, but far less than men.

The only other women I do not champion are those who are traitors to our gender and blame the victims of sexual assault rather than the perpetrators or very mistakenly insist women do not belong in the U.S. Military. Any woman in our Military is a hero, a patriot, and against all odds makes a disciplined soldier while doing something for the greater good of our country and citizens. Those who have proved themselves worthy as enlisted women must be rewarded with greater access to officer training to ensure that there will be enough women officers to lead and supervise current and future U.S. Military women.

Military men who question whether women have the emotional fortitude to succeed in the Military should examine their own high rate of PTSD, alcohol and drug problems, suicide, domestic violence and divorce. Yes, war is a very stressful occupation, even for macho men, but women have far fewer problems with binge drinking or drugs upon their return from the battlefield. "Thank You for Your Service" is the new movie being filmed now in Atlanta that is based on David Finkel's book of the same name about PTSD in returning Military personnel. And modern warfare is becoming more automated and less dependent on muscle and testosterone.

By way of further explanation, I offer my poem "Mirror Image & Something More." It is my challenge to both men and women—may we both live up to our responsibilities and greatest potential.

MIRROR IMAGE & SOMETHING MORE

Father, Brother, Uncle, Nephew, Husband, Boyfriend, and Sons:

Dismiss me if you dare. You'll be the first to look away. Eyes downcast you face our truth, and it is mighty. This is no *lie*. Women are for you, something more.

Mirror image of the best part of yourself, you cannot be a god without a goddess. There is no universe to master, for we are mistress of your destiny.

Leading the forces of good in the world, we stand directly in the path of evil. Brave beyond our bodies. We expect you to join us, fight with us—not against us and not among yourselves.

You're wasting valuable time in denial and defiance, when without our love, compassion, and nurturing spirit, there literally will be nothing to come home to. It's been a man's world, and its current state of implosion is on you.

Mother, Sister, Aunt, Niece, Wife, Girlfriend, and Daughters:

Command respect, plan your protection, and live up to your highest calling.

Or it's on us.

7

WHY MEN NEED WOMEN

G<small>UYS, YOU HAVE</small> got to get a good woman friend to advise you about women. She must be someone you have never been involved with romantically. Such a woman— perhaps a sister, a buddy's wife, or a college friend—can tell a man which women can be trusted and which ones aren't trustworthy.

These very necessary female advisors can also help a man get out of the "doghouse" with a girlfriend or wife when the man invariably misreads a situation or hurts a lover's feelings when he misspeaks.

May I also suggest that men cry when appropriate. When my roaring-tiger Dad crossed the line with those he loved, his remorse proved to me that it is a significant sign of strength and self-awareness. It is as good as confession for non-Catholics.

We all face demons when we look in the mirror, and maybe that is the beginning of humility because none of us is perfect. We are human after all, but if we refuse to straddle the fence, which men should avoid at all costs since it is especially painful on their private parts, we will never become demons and allow evil people to drag us into the tar pit at the entrance to Hell.

This is particularly true of sex which God gave us for our pleasure, or the human race would have died out long ago. We don't have to wallow in the mud to know it's there. Just smell the sulfur that rises when the devil stokes the fires. Sex without love is not gratifying or satisfying, it's not even good sex, and it leads to more frustration. Without love, sex is just the friction of body parts rubbing together. Pornography, sexting, sex clubs, and anonymous hookups have ruined many lives because decency and privacy disappear and it becomes an addiction.

Every man is different with every woman, and vice versa. That's why it is so special when a couple finds they are extremely compatible. But, men, take note, you cannot be a great lover if you are selfish in the bedroom. And those Viagra TV commercials are very scary for women as much as men when they say, "Half of men over 40 have some form of ED, or erectile dysfunction." No shame in getting help if it saves an intimate relationship. But all the Viagra in the world won't help you men if you don't learn that to get pleasure, you have to give pleasure. And that takes one-on-one time and your undivided attention.

And, young ladies, you must not suffer from the "easily distracted" syndrome of electronic social media. It makes you less experienced where it counts. It is up to you to give men the signal that you want to be kissed under the best of circumstances, such as slow dancing, when their arms are wrapped around you in a perfect embrace. The kiss will let you know if the chemistry is right, and a romantic relationship is worth pursuing.

And, ladies, please think twice before voluntarily or accidentally becoming some guy's "baby mama," unmarried mother of his child. Military women especially do not need to be unmarried and pregnant as it contradicts your desire to be a strong soldier. Use contraception or the new non-prescription morning after pill if you have to. Make sure Military pharmacies stock these items, and that your partners practice safe sex with you! That will show they respect you. And if they forced you to have sex, please report it. Be prepared to protect yourself.

Unfortunately, many young guys today take all romance out of the equation and instead perform sex in front of their friends to decide who to date, which is a sure sign of their own insecurity and narcissism and complete lack of empathy for the consequences to the girl, a fellow human being. They need to live the Hippocratic Oath as much as doctors—first, do no harm! Or karma will come up right behind you and bite you in the ass. Yes, it all comes down to morality, and it must be relearned.

I was a wife for 33 years, and I know most men need husband lessons—they must learn how to say "Yes, dear" and mean it even when they think they are right. My husband would argue that I wasn't right 100 percent of the time, so I challenged him to name the percent of my accuracy. After several rounds of obstinate denial, he finally had to admit I was right 99 percent of the time and had saved him much more often than he saved me. Try getting a Marine to admit that! When he whined about some messy situation he had stepped in, I'd say, "Adapt and overcome" (a Marine motto).

I also couldn't help pointing out two crucial observations: #1—Men spend entirely too much time watching sports on TV year-round—the Romans called it "bread and circus," i.e., feed and entertain the public, keep them fat and happy so they don't rebel; and #2—Most men cannot stand to be alone with themselves and their thoughts. That's why men really need women!

Okay, it took a woman to explain our national obsession for football. Diane Roberts, a tenured English professor at Florida State University (FSU), just published *Tribal: College Football and the Secret Heart of America*. A fierce Seminole fan all her life and FSU alumna, Dr. Roberts screams for blood at games right along with everyone else. It is because she cares so much for the game that she has put a lot of thought into the good and the bad of the sport, i.e., the magical nature of gridiron plays and the glorious dimension it adds to so many lives, counterbalanced by football players who commit rape for the most part with impunity—though FSU just had to pay $950,000 settlement and launch a re-education campaign because of a Title IX lawsuit brought by former student who said she was raped by their football quarterback—and the very real danger of traumatic brain injury.

NFL (football) players now say "NO MORE" to domestic violence and sexual assault as per the Super Bowl 50, February 7, 2016, commercial that advertised NoMore. org which is now the most active website to help the 12.7 million people who are physically abused, raped or stalked by their partners in 1 year in the U.S.

And now a caution for the hundreds of thousands of American men play Fantasy Football online with the hope of getting rich quick. Like Las Vegas, money-saving expert Clark Howard—clarkhoward.com—warns that the house always wins over time. Big-money investors have created this shark gambling opportunity to make themselves wealthy, not you. So much of the internet is a waste of time and money. Don't let it rob you of your common sense or your family and friends.

Watching the recent TV program *Cold Justice: Sex Crimes*, this shocking statistic appeared on the screen at the beginning of the show: There is a sexual assault every two minutes in the U.S.—a total of 290,000 per year. Again, 67 percent are fueled by drugs and alcohol. One clever American company is working on a clear nail polish that will turn colors if a woman dips her finger into a drink that has been drugged. Ten painted fingers could save the wearer and all her girlfriends in a bar. But this product is still in development.

The *Tinder* app popular among 18-24 year-olds has spawned a growing number of sexual assault complaints at police stations across our country. Young women, beware, 1,777 hookup requests does not make you popular or powerful. It makes you weak and a victim. Who are these guys? They photoshop a selfie and say they're a college student. But you'll never know for sure until it's too late. Weasels tell lies to steal what they want. Instead, choose a "bear" of a man who really likes and respects women. And Google or research them ahead of time. As the TV character Dr. Gregory House used to say, "Everyone lies." The Internet has just made it easier.

As further evidence of this, I offer the data breach by hackers of the "cheating spouse" website AshleyMadison. com announced August 18, 2015. Of the 32 million subscribers "outed," about 15,000 had U.S. Military or government email addresses. Guess they wanted to hide their infidelity from their wives—but how foolish was their use of Military email addresses when adultery is a punishable offense under the U.S. Uniform Code of Military Justice? By the way, there were 5 times as many men subscribers as women. Who were they going to be cheating with— each other? Admit it, fellas, women are not the problem— you are! Divorce lawyers predicted a lot of new business as wives searched the list of Ashley Madison subscribers and found their husbands' names. The *New York Times* said subscribers were already the victims of blackmail, identity theft, and other spinoff crimes—all for the thrill of doing something stupidly indiscreet.

One final thought for the gals: men need to be "tenderized" before they are any good in a relationship. My recommendation is that you let some other woman break them in first. Only after some heartache are they more aware of what it takes to have and maintain an equal partnership with you.

And all of us need to arrange our lives as we get older so that our weaknesses do not do us in.

8

GOOD LUCK
EQUALS RIGHT THINKING

TOO OFTEN WE complain about our bad luck when it is no worse than for everyone around us. How can we feel sorry for ourselves when the responsibility for wrong thinking—which is the source of all bad luck—is ours?

Right thinking is what we need at every intersection. Self-discipline is what we must achieve to become mature adults. There is no backsliding except into oblivion. Addicts consistently relapse and repeat rehab or treatment because they haven't gotten a grip on the cause of their illness, which in the final analysis is mental illness beyond depression, family dysfunction, or traumatic events—it also often includes an element of self-indulgence. Patrick Kennedy's new book *A Common Struggle: A Personal Journey through the Past and Future of Mental Illness and Addiction* is a revealing portrait of his life of drinking and drugging to cope with bipolar disorder and the many family secrets he had to keep as Ted Kennedy's son. He is a mental health advocate through his The Kennedy Forum.

Excessive drinking causes lasting damage to your brain including shrinking of the frontal cortex, reduced white matter which impair your ability to make judgments and control impulses. Online help kicking the alcohol habit or drug addiction is available online thru Reddit, i.e. r/ StopDrinking This kind of community and peer support is crucial to your recovery. Also, the scientific basis for hangovers means too much alcohol drunk too fast actually overloads your body with toxins, causing sleeplessness and nausea and whopping headaches making you unfit for duty or any kind of work.

You cannot feel too deeply or too much. Unlike most other animals, we are aware of right and wrong, kindness, and greed or grasping for what is not ours. Babies start out in life rewarding the generous puppet who shares his toys with their attention and smiles. It is only as babies grow older that they need socialization as children to learn again the traits of being nice.

Our only divine command is to be successful as human beings—first and foremost. If we fail in that, we've lost the whole ball game. If you hold on too tightly to an ever-increasing share of the pie in life, you end up living in fear that someone will take it away, especially if you're an impostor with a fake résumé.

MRIs done of the brains of avowed conservatives have overactive fear centers. Back to bravery—if you don't fear people, you can love them and by doing so, you can love yourself, your family, friends, and work colleagues—and everyone becomes special to you. What a life well lived you'll have.

I live by my own aphorism: "Trust to luck, but leave nothing to chance." That puts the outcome squarely on me where it belongs. Yes, I'm Italian and I believe in destiny, but I have never believed I am fated to lose. Neither is anyone else. I'm happy for you when you succeed. But allow me my own ideas of what it means to be successful in material terms. My aims are much higher.

9

BUSINESS

ONE OF MY favorite books is Dr. Robert I. Sutton's *No Asshole Rule*. One bad apple can and will spoil the whole workplace or Military installation. I passed this book to friends and family with wealthy but do-nothing partners used to a free ride. Getting rid of such partners is like getting a nasty divorce.

It's going to require strategic thinking—not necessarily more money to buy out the partner. And yes, it may require the services of an attorney whose demeanor is that of a bulldog. You want a lawyer who is as outraged as you are and who will fight for you as if you were his own kin.

Otherwise, hiring an attorney and expecting them to rescue you from your own bad decisions will be a big waste of money. You decide how you want to end the partnership—maybe by finding another investor to step up to the plate—and having your goal firmly in mind, devise a strategy that outsmarts your opponent. Your life is not a game to lose, even temporarily.

Disengage from the enemy so you can fight a better fight another day. This is not retreat—it is choosing your battles. It's not worth engaging the enemy head-on if you are not prepared. Think it through. Judges and courts are costly avenues of justice, and they may not favor common sense. But no one likes to reward a user. And please, to avoid the nasty surprise of a huge invoice from your attorney, make a deal to pay a flat fee—not an hourly, open-ended rate that could cost you an exorbitant amount of money per phone call.

For those of you wanting to start a business, watching *Shark Tank* on TV is invaluable. Imagine you have to explain your concept and work you've done to reach a sales goal to justify the often unrealistically high valuation people place on their ideas, products, or services. You must have a business plan and show profit, growth, and ROI (return on investment).

Most of the people who appear seem unprepared and take it very personally when the sharks rip apart their game plans. As in the *Survivor* and *Naked and Afraid* reality TV series, who would dare go to the jungle to test themselves if they weren't in shape? Similarly, you must be able to withstand the rigors of the jungle marketplace.

I will never forget the "theory of 10-80-10" in Ben Sherwood's book *The Survivor's Club*. In a crisis, 10 percent of people will assess the situation quickly and immediately take action and invariably are the first out and survive. These are the people you want to follow! Eighty percent of us will experience brain freeze for valuable moments, and we must learn to shake off the shock and move. When experienced skydivers fail to open their parachutes, it may simply have been this temporary analysis paralysis. The final 10 percent freak out, do the wrong thing, or just fatalistically stay in place and die. Avoid this at all costs.

If you are interested in buying an existing business, then you must determine exactly what you are buying. Is it good will, patented technology, a lucrative customer database, assets, etc.—and do these equate to the price? In business, bragging doesn't count on the balance sheet. Sometimes it makes more sense to start over on your own. And to learn how to think inside the box, read marketing whiz Linda Resnick's book *Rubies in the Orchard*, and discover her secrets behind the creation of top brands such as *Pom* pomegranate juice, *Fiji* bottled water, and *Teleflora*.

Franchise laws are very strict in the U.S., so let the buyer beware. Investors can be fickle, unreliable, and defy you to sue them. Noncompete clauses in a contract may be too broad and unenforceable. Make sure to trademark your invention. And be realistic about businesses which may have outlived their usefulness. As Amazon founder Jeff Bezos has said, "All businesses have a life cycle and eventually end and are overtaken by competitors."

For years, I've kept an "intuition journal" as recommended by Dr. Richard Wiseman in his book *The Luck Factor:*

The Four Essential Principles. Practice makes perfect, and consistently testing your intuitive powers by recording when they have actually saved the day gives you valuable milliseconds of advance insight in future dangerous situations. This is how experts become experts and can tell a fake from the real thing in the "blink of an eye," as per Malcolm Gladwell's book *Blink: The Power of Thinking without Thinking.* Mr. Gladwell is the well-known author of the invaluable book *Tipping Point,* which is a must-read for anyone marketing a product or service.

As an example, I had a car accident in my dear departed husband's car in June 2015 when it went out of control and jumped the curb at a high rate of speed, heading straight for a plate glass window and a hair salon full of ladies. The brakes did not work. I had to make a hard left to avoid the ladies, another hard left to avoid the brick pillar holding up the front of the shopping center, and a final hard left to avoid lots of parked cars. Miraculously, I was able to stop by pulling up the emergency brake and throwing it into park without injury and little damage. I got the car fixed but still did not feel safe driving it. Everyone thought I was chicken, but I didn't care, my intuition told me not to drive it. And three months later, I got a serious recall letter for my individual model and year saying the accelerator could stick and cause serious injury or death unless the dealer repaired the problem. They did, and on top of that, the car needed another $1,000 of brake repairs. Heavenly intuition saved me.

10

VIOLENCE, WOMEN & THE MILITARY

FORMER PRESIDENT JIMMY Carter's recent book *A Call to Action: Women, Religion, Violence, and Power* covers violence against women worldwide and the part he and his wife Rosalyn have played in overcoming these tragedies through their Carter Center in Atlanta. Page 116 of his book has a very shocking statistic—160 million women and girls have been wiped from the earth—a staggering number that is said to be the equivalent of losing two entire generations of women and girls in Asian countries, such as India, South Korea, China, etc., the Middle East, and Africa. The causes of death included selling of girls as child brides, too early pregnancies, the killing of baby girls or female fetuses, dowry killings, and genital mutilation.

Former President Carter, who was a submarine officer, also refers in his book to his days at the Naval Academy in Annapolis where sexual harassment and assault of women midshipmen was well-known and is still going on many decades later. The perpetrators of these offenses certainly are not qualified to become officers and lead or supervise others.

If Military Academy boys want to act like fraternity boys, let them go to a regular college! This kind of frat-house behavior has no place in the Military. And the officers who run these Military Academies should enforce discipline by making it the duty of every cadet to prevent sexual assaults by telling their buddies it's not cool, stop the crimes while they are happening, and report the incidents to faculty and administration. This is not snitching. This is doing your duty. And if you don't do your duty, demerits should follow.

I hope you will join your prayers with mine for the complete recovery of former President Jimmy Carter, who recently announced he has begun cancer treatment.

The *femicide* (gender killing) of so many women and girls, as per President Carter's book, has caused significant gender imbalance in Asia and Africa—i.e., more men than enough women to marry, and a resulting epidemic of sexual assaults, rapes, and gang rapes. By causing the death of so many women and girls, men are shooting themselves in both testicles. My husband and I saw the equivalent of this at the river where one lone scrawny female mallard duck would be escorted by a flotilla of bachelor males vying for her favors as a mate and mother.

But if this pitiful female tries to climb the riverbank to eat bread thrown by nature lovers, the male ducks attack her—not for sex—but to stop her from eating. It's self-defeating behavior that will not ensure the survival of their species or even a satisfying existence for the bachelors.

Ramifications of these types of anti-female acts done by men in colleges, the workplace, the Military, and in the home as domestic violence are dire and the outcome of a male-dominated culture that feels entitled to prey upon women. But it seems football players in particular, throughout the U.S., feel entitled to take women by force. If you are such big men on campus, why would you have to force a woman?

Is it any wonder that 1.5 million women and girls posted on Twitter that they felt under siege by men every day at #YesAllWomen within 24 hours of a horrible mass murder committed by a good-looking but deranged young California male student whose online manifesto said all women deserved to die because he was still a virgin and had never been kissed? These mostly young women shared tips on how to avoid dangerous confrontations with guys they didn't know who asked them for a date. There were two other murders in the news shortly after that fit this scenario—one by a 16-year-old boy who felt rejected by a high school girl who hardly knew him.

Women who have served in the U.S. Military did so with honor, medals, and promotions to General and

Admiral—though it took Army General Ann Dunwoody, the first woman 4-Star General in the Military, 60 years after women were first admitted to get this promotion. I read this in retired Navy Commander—and the first woman ever to take command of a Navy ship—Darlene M. Iskra's (PhD in Military Sociology) book *Women in the United States Armed Forces*, which details the many obstacles women face to promotion in all the services. Seeing her confident, competent, and beautiful on the cover of her book—which details the entire history of women in the Military—is inspiring to all women, especially qualified young American women we need to recruit.

In a book I just read from the local library about enlisting in the Army, it very clearly warns potential female recruits of the widespread danger of sexual assault and rape. Even so, qualified American women sign up and jump over many barriers. I say support and protect them, because if a fellow male soldier sexually assaults them and defiles the same uniform he's wearing, it's to me the equivalent of desecrating the U.S. flag which all soldiers swear to defend.

I know the Joint Chiefs say they need "bodies," but not criminals. Former chairman of the Joint Chiefs, General Martin Dempsey—after a scandal involving a male General—was quoted in the news as saying competence wasn't enough, that character counted just as much, if not more. Scandals are the "new morality" and the source of so many poor role models for young adults.

By now, many readers are wondering why I have such passion for reforming our Military—well, my main mission in life is always to improve the status of women. And personally, working on the issue of sexual assault on college and university campuses hits too close to home considering my experiences at Cornell having a fraternity boyfriend when there were 53 fraternities on campus and much bragging about their despicable behavior toward female students. I'll leave that crackdown to the Justice Department.

But I can be more objective about the Military and therefore, more effective. Besides, my uncle was a WWII Marine hero in the Pacific, my husband of 33 years was a Marine, and his father and grandfather Army. Another Uncle served in the Air Force, as did my Brother-in-Law. Maybe my WWII Navy Dad in Heaven is arranging this campaign of mine. I am not here to condemn the Military, but rather I am trying to help the Military come to grips with this problem. I'd like to salute all in the Military past, present, and future for protecting and defending us. Maybe it takes someone from the outside to see the big picture.

My Dad famously said to me when I was in my cap and gown at Cornell getting my BA—right in front of my boyfriend and his parents—with a slap on the back, a pumping handshake, and eye-of-the-tiger stare right into my eyes, "Now you're a man!" For a man born in the "old country"—Italy—where women really were second-class citizens, this was the highest compliment my Dad could pay any woman on earth. I had to take him aside and say, "Sorry, I'm all woman, but thank you for making me as fierce as any man because it had saved me several times at Cornell—and many more times in London."

Dad certainly knew how to motivate and incentivize. For years, when I didn't have a dime to my name, I carried with me a large signed portrait photo of him in profile looking exceptionally dashing in a tuxedo like the movie star Rudolph Valentino because of what he wrote in his large flamboyant handwriting at the bottom: "To my outstanding daughter, Anita, God love you. Dad." And then he signed it with his middle initial *R* as a five-pointed star with a circle drawn around it, almost as if it were a Sheriff's badge or a metaphysical symbol to protect against evil. I'm still trying to live up to it.

11

A WOMAN PRESIDENT

As I wrote in response to "likes" I received by direct e-mail to my "100 Million Votes" poem on YouTube.com, women need to feel it will be worth the fight to run for public office or join the Military. And a fight it will surely be.

Iceland had a "pots and pans" revolution after male bankers literally bankrupted the country with wild speculation in financial markets. The entire populace demanded more women in government and the financial industry. And in France, the only banks thriving during the recent Great Recession, which began in December 2007, were the banks run by women.

As the U.S. 2016 presidential election approaches, it is with chagrin that I realize that only one woman per political party, out of millions of educated American women, has declared her candidacy for the Democrats, Hillary Clinton, and one for the Republicans, Carly Fiorina. But a recent survey found that only 20 percent of Republican women would even vote for a woman president. GOP gals, you need to move your thinking to the 21st century.

What a truly sorry state of affairs for a country where women receive the same education as men from the age of 5. The last time my dear South Carolina friends brought their three young children for a visit, I made a point of talking to the two girls. Right in front of the parents and their younger brother, I asked the girls, "Do you take the same classes as boys? Do you have to take the same exams and get the same passing grades as boys? So you are just as smart and just as good as boys, aren't you? Don't let anyone tell you different, especially boys!" Their mother who is a certified teacher loved it. Even their brother agreed with it.

All it takes is for a good father to hold his baby daughter in his arms for the first time to realize he would do anything, not only to protect her but to help her fulfill every aspect of her destiny and talent. That's equal opportunity.

Do we all share this responsibility to our daughters and sisters? Yes, there is no way to shirk this responsibility to our side of the gender line. Not and walk our own spiritual path in this life with any honesty.

Women are quick to say that they've often been held back in the workplace by other women as well as men. Social psychological studies have shown that men have a harder time promoting more attractive women because they can't stop thinking of them sexually. It is plainer women who get promoted by men more often because they are less of a distraction. But why would other women sabotage members of their own gender? Is it jealousy, or simply that the traitors to their own gender are not as plugged into their own personal power?

To them, I suggest reading Clarissa Pinkola Estés, PhD, and Jungian psychologist's book *Women Who Run with the Wolves*. We are all like the poor little match girl dying in the snow who has to strike her last match for a tiny bit of heat and light. Pinkola Estés uses this mythic story to urge her women readers to "kick ass and come out fighting" when their back is pushed to the wall.

Yes, when faced with kidnapping by a Bluebeard, women may need a white knight to rescue them. But the gender of that knight under the armor could be male or female. Doesn't matter, for we are all our brother/sister's keeper on the road we all travel. This paraphrases M. Scott Peck's book *The Road Less Traveled*, which we early baby boomers took to heart.

But as Pinkola Estés and former President Jimmy Carter point out in their books, what we must do to prevent the years of bullying and physical attacks on women is to acknowledge that women are the source of everyone's life force and the creative principle for us all.

Here is my poem "100 Million Votes." This book is the only place you will find the words of my free verse poems printed out for you.

100 MILLION VOTES

Whisper it woman to woman…and man to man… chant it, *will* it into being…shout it as a group until every eligible voter in America makes it real—our first woman president of the United States in 2016.

Almost 100 years since white women got the vote in 1920 and 50 years since women of color did too with the Voting Rights Act of 1965. Even black men got the vote many decades before us—in 1870 with the 15th Amendment to the Constitution. God knows it is our turn.

We don't want a *man*date, we want a *woman*date. Not a landslide, a *woman*slide for every American woman, and every other girl & woman worldwide. And let's make it a double victory with a woman VP as well.

Men, show us your gratitude, your respect, your belief we are your equals. Look your wives and daughters in the eye and tell them *why you wouldn't* vote for a woman president. If it's one thing men have taught us, it's that if you don't ask, you don't get. So we're asking for it all—the 100 million votes cast in the last presidential election.

Men are also fond of telling women there will be consequences if we don't follow orders. Well, if we don't get our double presidential victory, I hereby give permission for every woman & girl to take the next day off to rest and recharge. I did not say we won't spend money. We'll just spend it on ourselves. And everyone will see how valuable our contribution is to society.

Every man is born of woman—your flesh & blood & breath of life came from ours. So I need three promises from men: #1—Police yourselves & other men & boys to honor rather than abuse women & girls; #2—Stay out of "women's issues" and let us control our own bodies; and #3—Free the last great group of slaves by supporting an "underground railroad" to rescue abused women & girls. You do this, and you'll be the heroes of a happy home, and we'll take care of the house—the White House & House of Congress!

12

WOLF OF WALL STREET

ASKING A WISE woman friend to answer the question "What would the world be like without women?" She said, "It wouldn't last long!" Now that's truth because we all know, after seeing the movie *Wolf of Wall Street*, men left entirely to their own devices would soon descend into the most deplorable kind of locker-room, all-boys-club behavior.

It could not be said about the movie "that no women were harmed in the production of this film." More care is taken to put this disclaimer on films involving animals. But in this movie, the men kept their pants on while the women—even the beautiful, statuesque blonde female star—were wide-open naked to the camera during scene after scene of simulated fornication.

Yet, I applaud director Martin Scorsese and his male leads, Leonardo DiCaprio and Jonah Hill—all three of whom were nominated for Academy Awards—for portraying the depths of depravity our Wall Street stock traders reach while gambling with our life savings. It was extremely brave of these three men to show their gender at its worst.

Leonardo DiCaprio, who just received an Academy Award as Best Actor for his new film *The Revenant,* was quoted in Parade magazine January 10, 2016 issue as saying: "Women have been the most persecuted people throughout all of recorded history, more than any other race or religion." Thank you, Leo, for stating this truth better than I ever could.

But I knew they would never win those Hollywood awards because of the blatant denigration of women as depicted in the real Jordan Belfort *Wolf of Wall Street*'s book. Seeing the author interviewed on TV, I realized he was a mini-Bernie Madoff who went to jail for only two years for bilking thousands of innocent people so he could pay for his lavish lifestyle and snort copious amounts of cocaine. Now he teaches seminars—only in America can a little nerd, cokehead, defiler of women who punched his wife and endangered his own baby daughter make more money for his crimes by teaching seminars.

As Marilyn vos Savant—Mensa brilliant columnist for *Parade* magazine, which has an audience of 33 million readers in everyone's Sunday newspaper in the U.S.— explained in a column, you have no control over the companies your money is being invested in, and you know little about their directors or problems that may not have hit the news yet. Not unless you're an inside trader who is profiting from privileged information which can get you sent to jail like Martha Stewart, who only did what her stockbroker told her to do.

But not only does insider trading happen in more cases than we're aware of but high-speed stock trades done by computers to gain milliseconds of advantage for the large investment firms that use them further disadvantage you. This makes investing in stocks gambling—pure speculation—as Robert B. Reich, former labor secretary under Bill Clinton, and White House financial advisor, noted author, and professor at the University of California, Berkeley, is quick to point out in his book *Aftershock* and major motion picture *Inequality for All*. Only 12 percent of Americans even own stocks, and the richest 5 percent of Americans own 82 percent of all stocks. For years during the Great Recession, the Federal Reserve was spending $85 billion per month to prop up our economy after Wall Street crashed and almost bankrupted our country in 2008.

The top 1 percent of earners can afford to gamble in the stock market because they have more money than they can spend. And they'd rather gamble their money away instead of doing good works to help the less fortunate like Warren Buffet's group of billionaires who've taken his "Giving Pledge" to donate $500 million (half of a billion dollars) of their wealth to charity. Most wealthy Americans feel no obligation to follow in the generous footsteps of Henry

Ford, Andrew Carnegie, or Bill Gates who left and are leaving a legacy of caring for their fellow man and woman. No need to wonder why it's written in the Bible that it's harder for the rich to get into Heaven.

Robert Reich just published, September 2015, a new book titled *Saving Capitalism: For the Many, Not the Few*, in which he takes our nation's economic structure to task. *Publisher's Weekly* magazine praised the book as "arresting, thought provoking" and ranks it one of the top 10 business and economic releases. Sounding much like Pope Francis, Mr. Reich says in its current unchecked state, capitalism is at the heart of ballooning and inexcusable inequality. He shatters entrenched myths about capitalism and offers us an accessible and riveting guide.

On Christmas Day 2015 I went to a packed showing of the new movie "The Big Short" that explained how Wall Street through greed, stupidity and fraud created the 2008 mortgage crisis that brought down the entire U.S. economy. The fallout was that 8 million people lost their jobs, 6 million people lost their homes and our country lost $5 trillion of wealth. The beautiful blonde star, Margot Robbie, of Wolf of Wall Street explained how CDO's Collateralized Debt Obligations based on fraudulent mortgage backed securities were the cause. Yet Wall Street had the nerve to blame the poor and immigrants and are committing this same fraud again under a different name. Michael Lewis who wrote the book "The Big Short" recommends using IEX which has applied to be its own stock exchange in Atlanta because they can compete honestly with high speed traders on Wall Street. The next big commodity crisis is predicted to be WATER. See the final chapter in my book Full Circle.

13

POLITICS—MY PARTY

When asked, I say my political party is Mother Theresa—I'm for all the people all the time—except for evildoers, of course.

Readers will have already classified me as a liberal, and so I am. When I wrote my valedictory speech in high school, I chose the topic moral complacency and dared to use hateful words to talk against racism, anti-Semitism, ethnic slurs, misogyny (hostility toward women), etc. I thought there would be a huge backlash of complaints by parents and teachers listening in the stands of the old football stadium. But no one ever said a word against me. I believed it might be the last time I got to address a large audience and must speak truth. I could not have known that public speaking would become my life's work for 33 years in Atlanta.

In Dan Brown's subsequent book to his blockbuster *The Da Vinci Code* called *Inferno*, he focuses on the greatest sinners in Dante's 9th level of Hell who are forced to face

Satan directly. Worse than child molesters in Dante's epic poem of Heaven and Hell (*Inferno*) are "those who fail to take action in a moral crisis." I told my very Christian and wonderful Aunt Rose I have never been and will never be guilty of that sin.

Much to my dear departed husband Michael's consternation, I would stand up and verbally slap back across the line they crossed, any foul-mouthed abuser of women and children. I waited for the men to stop these terrible people in Mexico, Jamaica, or Atlanta, and when they didn't step in, I did. I was called "magnificent" at the baggage claim or given a round of applause, but I didn't do it for that. I asked the men why they didn't intervene and was told "it would have come to blows."

Why? I did it with my big mouth—I was a teacher of wine-drinking adults for decades and am admittedly bossy as a result—and a great entertainer or I wouldn't have been able to impart the huge amount of knowledge in my course book. Talk about having to keep control of a crowd! And I am an "intimidator" personality type—we know we're stronger than most people since we have tested our limits countless times. So I am "granny with a gun, without the gun." When I said this to one friend, he said, "Anita, you're the pistol."

Recently, I shared my ideas for the Military with a retired Army Colonel who called me "colorful." He categorized me correctly. While at Cornell, I was a volunteer for

Planned Parenthood and was the one sent to demonstrate contraceptive devices because little embarrassed or frightened me when I was doing good works. I also was one of 3 women students at Cornell on the original committee with 3 women faculty to create the first women's studies course in the U.S. there in 1969.

And at the height of the AIDS epidemic in Atlanta, I volunteered to speak to the most hostile and homophobic groups in memory of gay men friends who had died of the disease. Once I was locked in a room with 30 bus drivers down at their depot and in one hour was able to convert them to compassion and tolerance. That's when I truly understood that God had me in training all my life to be able to do that.

I became a writer because every week during summer vacation, I checked out 10 books to read from the elementary school library. The librarian questioned my ability to comprehend the more advanced books since I was only in 4th grade. She quizzed me on *Gulliver's Travels*, and I told her I was little but not Lilliputian in my ambition. That came from my Dad who started teaching me about money, people, and life from the time I was 7 years old.

The money lesson really took hold—Dad had received a big check for his share of the sale of his parents' home in Connecticut and cashed it at the bank. He sent everyone else away and spread out that big bundle of cash on the table in front of me and said, "Count it." I could hardly count past ten, let alone into the thousands. He told me this was not play money, that it had to be worked for, and that it was what put food on the table and would send me and my sisters and brother to Catholic school. He helped me count that money. And then he called back my Mom and gave her every last dollar to pay off the mortgage on our house. That was the real money lesson.

Cash is king. You will only have so many "earning" years. And that number of years can be shortened through circumstances beyond your control, such as a downturn in the economy or job loss, injury from accidents, or long-term illness. After my husband lost his job to company downsizing in 2011, we were saved by his severance package and the fact that he had reached full retirement age and could begin collecting Social Security and go on Medicare.

Beware—it is not true that you lose money if you start to claim Social Security at age 66—my husband was dead by age 69 and would have missed years of payments if he had waited. His 401K, which he had been paying into for 11 years with money deducted directly from every paycheck before he could spend it, had actually gone down dramatically when the company stock price plummeted. After he died in 2014, what saved me was the life insurance policy he carried over from work.

I laugh when well-to-do friends say they must "make their money work for them" by investing in the stock market. Money doesn't work for you—you work to earn it! Or it was earned by some relative who left it to you as inheritance. Everyone I know lost tens of thousands of dollars they could little afford to lose in the Great Recession. And millions of Americans lost their biggest asset—their homes—to foreclosure caused by Wall Street overspeculation. Even now at the end of 2015, 20 percent of Atlanta area homes are still "underwater," meaning owners owe more on the mortgage than the house is worth. That money has never been recouped by the middle class. Only the rich got richer. But it is calculated that the rich hide from U.S. taxes by sheltering it overseas to the tune of $32 trillion dollars—much greater than our national debt of $19 trillion.

Congressmen may scream about this national debt, but they became millionaires after they arrived in Washington because of privileged information they use to invest in and profit from the stock market. Yet no Congressman has ever been charged with insider trading. Sure, there are ethics laws, but they are seldom enforced for this day-to-day business as usual. And we're the suckers who keep them in office with our votes. Most of the political women are blameless, however, since there are so few of them holding elected office in Washington—only 20 senators out of 100 are women, and that's the highest it's ever been.

Thank God we ordinary citizens each have a vote. That fact is the one irritant to plutocrats—the wealthy who want to turn our democracy into a plutocracy run by the rich. We outnumber them with our votes. This is why certain state politicians have tried so hard to disenfranchise the poor and middle-class voters—especially minorities. Use your vote or lose it! And think for yourselves by questioning politicians' motives. If you live in Detroit or Baltimore or certain California cities, your city actually went bankrupt as part of the fallout from the Great Recession. And so far, none of the traders who perpetrated these abuses has been jailed. You can rent Michael Moore's documentary movie *Capitalism: A Love Story* to get a history lesson in how all this unfolded.

Michael Moore's new movie *Where to Invade Next* just released at the end of 2015 is being praised as a hilarious, heartfelt plea for the U.S. to adopt some of the best solutions to our problems that other countries found to be very effective.

Tax cheats and immoral "wolves of wall street" are not patriots. How can their actions possibly show love of our country? Someone quoted a bumper sticker to me that said, "The rich convince the middle class to blame the poor." That must have been how rich Southern plantation owners got white overseers to whip their black slaves, when genealogy has proven those plantation owners would rather have mated with the slaves than intermarry with poor whites.

What surprises me is that very few Southerners are aware that the "peonage" system of throwing young black men into chain gangs to provide free labor for local counties or farmers went on for 100 years after the Emancipation Proclamation that freed the slaves. The Civil Rights movement finally brought that to an end. Even so, over 1.5 million young black men from the South joined the U.S. Military to fight in WWII after President Truman signed an executive order in 1942 to allow this. Ask yourself, would you have been so forgiving or so honorable?

As I reference in my poem "Holding Hands—Metaphysics," mitochondrial DNA traces us genetically to the first Eve, the mother of all of us humans on earth—a woman of the African race. Now patrilineal DNA can be traced back to the father of all of us—a black man from East Africa. Go back far enough in time, and you'll see we really are "brothers/sisters in arms"—and I don't mean just as soldiers. Men, as #1 *New York Times* best-selling action writer James Rollins pointed out in his book *The Eye of God*, you may be among the 1 in 200 men living today who can trace their biological heritage to the Mongolian world conqueror Genghis Khan. He and his male relatives took full advantage of the women as spoils of war.

By the way, I wrote "Holding Hands—Metaphysics" for my friend Nancy who was teaching a high school Advanced Placement class on Human Geography. I joked with her that it sounded like the study of the erogenous zones of the human body. But of course not! It was the study of human migration and its causes and how we ended up spread over the earth. Her high school students loved my poem even before I performed it on YouTube and dedicated it to them. They called it "awesome" and said please add their applause to my worldwide audience. I don't have one yet, but I realize how hard it is to impress teenagers. I replied back to them that they must aim as high as their imaginations.

One last note on the subject of money—one of Anita's aphorisms—"If you are the one who makes the deposit in the universal piggy bank, i.e., creates something worthwhile, then you have earned the right to make the withdrawal." So never worry about the competition or what other people are doing, and don't infringe someone else's copyright, create your own wealth by doing something that benefits everyone. Every bridge, fantastic building, or beautiful work of art came from the mind of man. Put your own higher mind to work for you, protect your intellectual property rights, and then build an even better mousetrap— your own version 2.0.

HOLDING HANDS—METAPHYSICS

Harmony converged in the park August 16–17, 1987, as we gathered worldwide to take the hands of strangers and make a circle of unity around the globe.

Imagine the energy of this human "God particle" generator as we held tight for peace. Surprising who was on either side of us—everyone. Reconnected and proving what separates us are false beliefs, not distance, religion, or tribe.

Be there, or be part of the problem.

No one wanted to be the first to let go.

Cynical was not an option, because we could see the long line of ancestry that placed us on earth.

Threads of time, of DNA, from the Mother of us all out of Africa, lower mind and higher mind are in our makeup throughout the history of war, migration, feast, and famine. Survival has always required cooperation and, yes, charity.

Be an island if you choose, we must all go to that mountaintop for wisdom. But then what good is there if it isn't shared?

Don't hold on to riches, but to each other, or we may end up clutching ashes instead of enlightenment.

14

ALL FAMILIES ARE DYSFUNCTIONAL

AN ASTROLOGER FRIEND, Fran Rackow, once used my natal (birth) chart and a 3-hour interview for a report to other certified astrologers on how a person can take the potential they were born with and maximize the most positive aspects of it to the fullest. This friend was a graduate of my Wine School in Atlanta, had traveled with my group to Tuscany, and forever after called me a "star." But what impressed her about my life when referring back to the astrological map of the heavens at the time and in the place I was born was that I had taken the God-given talents indicated, and overcoming the difficult aspects, had become a wildly skillful and greatly self-actualized person. My chart said "nuclear power" potential—and I made it personal power.

I also had the degree of Bacchus (god of wine) on my ascendant or rising sign—and this baby girl made wine her career for 35 years. I also have Venus (goddess of love and beauty, my ruler) and Mars (leading all the other planets like an engine) together in my house of career—foretelling my own militancy and work surrounded by men, while never losing my femininity.

The "fault is not in our stars." Some of the most accomplished people past and present had very tough childhoods. I did. So much so that I tried to run away from home at age 6, and my astrologer friend actually saw this in my chart. Of course I didn't get very far—I scribbled a good-bye note to my parents and made it out into the street before I realized I didn't have any money for the bus. I had to be patient and wait until I was 18 to leave home for college. But having a large, loud, dysfunctional Italian family gave me motivation to find a way to empower myself and leave on the best of terms.

I believe in astrology because I earned a living from it when I worked part-time for "Astrologer to the Stars" Frederic Davies in London. Celebrities routinely came to the door, and I helped write his *London Evening News* astrology column and the personality profiles of his famous clients. It was among his old books that I first became a student of metaphysics—there was even an entire book on Soulmates that explained there are several different kinds, not just romantic. And that the ultimate Soulmates were equal partners on all levels, but especially on the spiritual level, who moved mountains for Heaven.

My family taught me unconditional love. As the firstborn child, I was expected to help the adults and act like one. When, at age 9, I found my Mother lying in bed in a pool of blood, I was ordered to find my Dad to take her to the hospital, keep my two sisters from knowing anything was wrong for a whole day and night by myself, and keep this secret of my Mother's miscarriage from the rest of the family, which I did for 50 years. At the time, I didn't even know what a miscarriage was, and I couldn't cry or show fear in front of my younger sisters—even though I was scared to death that my Mother was dying. And that was the same year my Grandfather died, and my parents mistakenly took me to the funeral where I promptly fainted from seeing a dead body for the first time.

Perhaps the greatest criticism that can be leveled against an Italian American is laziness. That is disrespecting and dishonoring an ethnic group whose immigrant sons and daughters helped build America—especially New York City from the ground upward—with their bodies and blood. Their story was movingly illustrated in the novel *Elizabeth Street* by Laurie Fabiano. I was always proud to be an Italian American, as was my high school covaledictorian who lived just a few doors down the street. It wasn't until best-selling author Lisa Scottoline had a copy of her grandparents ID card from the shameful internment of poor Italian Americans in camps during WWII that I learned that our people had shared a fate similar to Japanese Americans, while our Dads and Uncles fought in the war.

As for my covaledictorian in high school, Ray LeClair, both our mothers were born in the same picturesque hill town of Monsampolo (Mount St. Paul) in Marche, Italy, overlooking vineyards and farmland that cascaded down limestone cliffs to the azure-blue Adriatic Sea. The people are industrious and gentle—treasured family whose heritage made me a lover of nature and left me a legacy of unshakable faith in the goodness of people that has allowed me to help others avoid stepping into pain.

When I returned to Monsampolo with my husband Michael, Aunt Rose, and Cousin Nancy, I knew it was my mother in Heaven who arranged for us to witness a divinely inspiring ceremony of nuns in nurse uniforms with huge winged caps pushing patients in wheelchairs to be blessed with holy water by a priest while doves flew in a circle overhead and altar boys spread incense. This was outside the church at Loreto in Ancona, which houses a life-size statue of St. (Padre) Pio, a breathtaking gold-encrusted sacristy, and the Shrine of the Black Madonna, whose face has been blackened by the soot of candles lit by the faithful for generations. I believe it is a message against racism for everyone who dares practice it in the name of God or any religion.

To give my siblings credit where it is most definitely due, they inherited the same "salt of the earth" characteristics from our family past and present. My sister has been married for 48 years, and she and her husband have given us a family life we would never have had because of her two children and grandchild. My brother has been with his wife over 38 years, and I was married for 33 years. It is not just that we were raised Catholic and don't believe in divorce. We are loyal, and family means everything. Families may cause us pain, but we go back because they understand us better than anyone else. And if they don't, then do what my hairdresser Ray Sloot told me: "Maybe it's time to cut the dead branches from the family tree."

In Geoff Colvin's book *Talent Is Overrated: What Separates World Class Performers from Everybody Else*, myriad examples are offered that to become a "legend" in your field—whether music, sports, science, teaching, or business—you must invest a minimum 10,000 hours of practice. We may have talent, but to make that talent a skill will take huge amounts of hard work above and beyond the norm.

If I am able to sense the mood of an audience in the first 15 seconds, think of something funny to say to get them to plug into me, levitate them off their chairs with fascinating knowledge, become their guru for life because I made it the fastest and most fun two hours of their lives, and then wow them at the end with a song—it's because I've done it thousands of times.

No one, certainly not a woman, had ever earned 4 income streams at once in Atlanta in the wine business—and no one has replicated this since then. I worked full-time in the wine industry at the retail, wholesale, and import levels; was wine writer every month for 5 years for *Atlanta* magazine, and then every month for 5 years at *Atlanta Homes and Lifestyles* magazine (among several other publications); was online wine expert for CNN.com; taught well over 2,000 wine courses in my own wine school for hotels, restaurants, the wine trade, and the public—each course 6-8 weeks long using my own course book; performed hundreds of wine parties and events in Atlanta and from Las Vegas to Bermuda; was leader of wine tours to France and Italy; and published *Pick a Perfect Wine...In No Time* with Que Publishing—still available on Amazon where it received 5 Star ratings and is a complete wine course readable in one sitting.

People in the wine business who had never seen me perform said I was "too good to be true," but I was true. I have file drawers full of evaluations in their own handwriting from people who were in my audiences. But no one knew that I won a nationwide video talent search by E & J Gallo's ad agency (at the time, Young & Rubicam) but turned them down when they wanted me to quit a high-paying wine job with no income guarantee from them.

Or that I was signed to a contract by the Sr. VP of Robert Mondavi Winery (without Mr. Robert Mondavi's knowledge) who then reneged on it and cost the winery a million dollars when the wine center project I put on paper for them failed miserably at Disney Los Angeles and closed in 8 months without me. Or that I received a lifetime of good will from Mr. Robert Mondavi and Brice Cutrer-Jones of Sonoma-Cutrer winery for helping them and 48 other wineries sue and win against their own California wine marketing board. That marketing board made the big mistake of asking me to fly to California at my expense to present 5 proposals which they, without my permission, sent out to 60 wineries and then squandered their budget on someone else's horribly embarrassing commercials. Evildoers, try to remember never to screw a journalist. It is our duty to be whistleblowers.

Conclusion: are you a man or woman who knows your worth? If you try to use me as a doormat and complain that I didn't remove the mud from your boots, watch out! I'll bite your ankle off. Funny, some of the old gentlemen of Atlanta's wine business e-mail me now to say how much they respected me as the only woman among them. Well, it's never too late to acknowledge that a woman is your equal.

Nature is what really recharges my batteries. The following poem "River Leaves & Muskrat Stillness" flows like the river where I practiced open-eyed meditation when times were tough. A dear friend in England said she "floated down the river with me" and called me a clever gal. It is my reminder to all of you to take time away from your computer and phone to hear the real Master's voice. And yes, this did happen with the Muskrat. It could have been a river otter, but I was told by the local park ranger that it was a Muskrat and they love to eat the small river clams, as does the rare mink, and more numerous raccoons. Try to be as still as I was—that's how the Indians hunted. They became part of nature.

RIVER LEAVES & MUSKRAT STILLNESS

Family pain through the alchemy of writing turned into art. Financial crisis overturned, but only with nature as the midwife.

It's autumn, and leaves are falling from the crimson, burgundy, orange, and neon-yellow trees into the river. Some leaves are big and flat, making a splash like skipping stones. Seemingly efficient rafts navigating the swift stream, they are soon sunk by the curling waves of rushing white water.

Other leaves having *duck* shapes expertly float, bobbing up and down as they swim for their lives in the swift current. Although taking the first dips of the rapids well, unlike real ducks, they become waterlogged, completely losing their shape and buoyancy. The only ones of their kind who make it down the river adapted by changing their profile.

Smaller, less impressive leaves proved to be the master helmsmen, steering closer to shore as the river tried its best to batter them. But by taking the slower route closer to the bank, they made it all the way downstream. Lessons whispered to me by the breeze.

Reward for this stillness, my superpower, is the companion who climbs out, dripping wet, onto the rock beside me. Impossibly red-haired Muskrat with a vertical flat tail sits calmly eating shellfish and then begins grooming.

15

MY HUSBAND— JEWELED BUTTERFLY

PEOPLE WHO CRITICIZE immigrants to the U.S. forget that we were all immigrants. Only Native American Indians have rightful claim to our country since they were the original settlers. My husband Michael was descended from both the pilgrims who came over on the Mayflower, and the Wampanoag Indians. They were the Thanksgiving Indians of Cape Cod who helped save the starving pilgrims and then were murdered for their land down to the last great Wampanoag chief, King Phillip, "The Red King," whose wife and son, after his death, were enslaved by the colonists. Imagine being a mash-up of the two.

We owe millions of dollars of restitution to Native American tribes who were marched off their land at gunpoint and cheated out of their mineral rights royalties by our government's Bureau of Indian Affairs in the 19th century. Indian reservations became "refugee camps" with incredibly high rates of unemployment and alcoholism. Don't cry for them—their pride and accomplishments won't allow for it. But please keep in mind what we still owe them as a nation. After Barak Obama became president, he was finally able to see that their lawsuits against our government would get settled, and Native American tribes danced in his inaugural parade and a National Museum of the American Indian was established in Washington, DC.

My husband was a real "rainbow child." Though his birth certificate says his color was Red Indian and one of his two Irish great-grandmothers was a Mayflower descendant, his maternal grandfather was from the West Indies and of African descent. Born very blonde and blue-eyed, his almost hairless red skin and aquiline nose gave him a very exotic look that he said caused every little girl in school when he was growing up to swoon over him—and lots of big girls too later in life. The following poem "Jeweled Butterfly" is my tribute to him and his passing. The only things I left out were what baseball team he played third base for and that he was a Marine. We were semper fidelis. He said I was tough enough to be a Marine but not mean enough.

JEWELED BUTTERFLY

Three angel children sang "Michael rowed the boat ashore, hallelujah, when his health began to fail and he had to trim his sails, hallelujah."

Himself a Cape Cod boatman, he was flown to Heaven by the spirit of the WWII pilot who had lived next door. The vision seen by our new neighbor at the moment Michael crossed to the other side, 1:00 AM—God's, the great "I Am," hour.

He marched on Washington with Martin Luther King Jr., watched Jimi Hendrix at Woodstock, played chess and baseball like a champ, spun jazz as a radio DJ in Boston, and managed thousands of programming change requests at work.

But his greatest achievements were giving back the boat he inherited to save a family and the gentleness with which he massaged his Mother's feet and manicured her nails as she lay for years with MS in a nursing home.

All races wanted to claim him—his birth certificate and smooth red skin said he was Native American—Wampanoag, the Thanksgiving Indians. But his blue eyes and blonde hair were likely from the Irish great-grandmother whose forebears descended from the famous ship Mayflower.

AAO—Against All Odds, he twice overcame personal childhood devastation to become the beautiful soul whose passing caused people to cry openly, even in the grocery store. If only he could have lived to see how much they loved him.

My jeweled butterfly for 33 years, Michael was the iridescent light shining on the copper of an antique saxophone in the Easter sun or through a church's stained glass window. He was a prism refracting white light into the color spectrum VIBGYOR—violet, indigo, blue, green, yellow, orange, red. Friends said, "Anita without Michael is unfathomable."

The last TV program we watched together was *Cosmos*, hosted by Neil DeGrasse Tyson and written by the late Carl Sagan's equally brilliant wife Ann Druyan. They explained we are all made of "star stuff." That's where everyone on earth originated—the stars. If only we would act like it.

16

ROARING-TIGER DAD

IT TOOK MY Italy-born father 13 years to get U.S. citizenship, even though he and his family owned and worked a combination retail store and soda fountain in Torrington, CT. Other owners now have a newsagent on the main street there that still bears the LaRaia name. If my Dad hadn't been a U.S. citizen, he would never have been allowed to join the U.S. Navy Reserve at nearly 40 to go to sea on a destroyer in the North Atlantic during WWII. With his dog tags, my brother found a hand-typed, hand-signed letter from the President thanking Dad for his service.

He was Chief Steward and the morale of the ship whose sailors and officers were half his age. He showed me his menus—beans, beans, beans—and had nothing but powdered eggs, powdered milk, flour, salt, a little sugar, etc., to impress the captain and crew. When anyone had a birthday or something to celebrate, he'd make a cake and "champagne" from golden raisins in a crock. All while German planes fired from above and torpedoes were aimed at them from below. Now you know why he was so popular that the officers brought him to their hometown in Pennsylvania after the war to meet and marry my 24-year-old Italy-born farm girl and opera singer mother.

Being a Navy man, Dad had no trouble getting Mom to accept his marriage proposal, but her father—a Field Marshall in WWI Italy—was 6 foot 4 inches of unsmiling dissent. I used to have to curtsy and kiss his hand every Sunday as a little girl and stare him down until his hard green eyes softened. The Italian men still called him Field Marshall because many of them had immigrated to the U.S. after WWI with him and worked under him when he became foreman of the steel mill. It took over 15 years for him and the other Italian men to save enough money to send for their wives and children. Nonno (Italian for grandfather) kept the steel mill running for the WWII war effort and got my tiny 5-foot-1-inch Mother to forge steel too. My nonna (Italian for grandmother) was just as tough—she raised my Mother, worked the farm in Italy, and took care of her elderly parents all by herself for the 15 years she waited for her husband to send for her and my Mother. Then she had two more children with him in the U.S.

In my poem "White Roses & Pussy Willows," I refer to my Dad as a "roaring tiger," and he was. Born in 1902, a year of the tiger in Chinese astrology—the most ferocious, dangerous, and rarest of the 12 animal signs. Dad was not very tall, but he could make the hair on the back of your neck stand on end just by entering the room. His presence and personality were huge, and he could literally bring an explosion of life force into any human situation. I can too, but I learned not to throw my weight around like he did. Yet he was the favorite brother among his siblings and the favorite uncle of our many first cousins, a man's man but very generous. He was shocked to realize that I, his firstborn baby daughter, had his fearlessness—proving we inherit more than eye and hair color from our parents but personality traits as well. I was raised by tough guys—and gals—and am just like them as a result.

But I'm also a "warrior angel" doing my heavenly and earthly duty—just like most of our brave soldiers of both sexes.

When I was a little girl, I was told I was as stubborn as my paternal grandmother who was revered in the family as a holy woman with a fierce disposition from having moved her husband and family (she eventually had seven living children) from Italy to Argentina and then the U.S. She had the gift of prophecy and would make my Dad open the Bible so she could point to passages that she said gave the answer to the many heated family discussions.

My maternal Grandmother used to ask me to walk her to one of her dear woman friends from the old country so they could share a small glass of the golden sweet Italian herbal liqueur Strega, which means "witch" in Italian. To be a smart-aleck, I asked the very religious old ladies why they would drink something with a black witch on the bottle. And they answered that there are bad witches but also good witches too and that it was okay to use things like the phases of the moon for planting, predicting births, and decisions. They gave me permission to be the good witch I am.

My Dad wasn't the only LaRaia to go to war. His younger brother Caesar—a very tall, extremely handsome guy—was a Marine who was dropped on a Pacific island to fight the Japanese, virtually unaided and with few supplies, for four years during WWII. He got malaria, what would many years later be known as PTSD, and a bunch of medals for his perseverance.

This jungle experience was not the first for our LaRaia men. My paternal great-Grandfather left Italy with his two young boys after his wife died to travel to Venezuela in the early 1900s to trade with the Indians for gold. Confirmation of these remarkable family stories came when I took an anthropology course at Cornell and the professor told me his *mestizo* (mixed blood, white and Indian) guide in Venezuela that summer had Dad's full name, including a most unusual spelling of his middle name Rocco (Rock).

When I returned to my dorm after that class, I called my Dad, and he admitted that his Grandfather, the widower, did indeed marry an Indian woman in Venezuela when he was there trading for gold with his young son, my Dad's father. The other son stayed in South America—my Great Uncle Pedro and became an architect and a rancher in the Pampas. That's why my Dad grew up and went to school in Argentina as a boy after leaving Italy and before the U.S. My Dad and his two sisters spoke several languages including Spanish, and perhaps that's why I was given the name Anita. Although years later, I found a photo signed with love to my Dad from a Spanish dancer named Anita. My Mom didn't seem to care—I always said she was a saint for putting up with Dad.

What my LaRaia ancestors gave the Venezuelan Indians in exchange for the gold were iron farm implements from a foundry in Torrington, CT. How my Italian great-grandfather even knew about ordering goods from America in the early 1900s is a mystery. But years later when my Dad and his family disembarked at Ellis Island, our history came full circle when they told the customs inspectors they were going to Torrington, CT! And to think I married a man of Indian descent.

17

SUM TOTAL

WE ARE ALL the sum total of our heritage and experience. My direct male lineage included these "ramas of the jungle," which made me realize how themes repeat themselves throughout our lives. My first cousin Tony has as evidence the 100-year-old hammock—restored by his mother Aunt Marie—that our Grandfather learned to weave so he could sleep above the ground like the Indians in the Venezuelan jungle.

That cousin—who I hadn't seen in 50 years—said my Dad was a most attentive uncle. As young boys, they would come running when my Dad drove up in his American-made Graham automobile. Only 72,000 Graham autos were made in Detroit by three American brothers who patented the first cars with truck chassis. They also won an award for developing the amphibious vehicles that brought our troops to Normandy beach during WWII. Leave it to my Dad to have such a cool car.

I will never be guilty of hypocrisy, I tell my Aunt Rose, because I've put my life where my big mouth is. If I believe in the equality of man, I lived it by marrying a man of many races. My husband and I would often ask ourselves why God would bring us to Georgia where even friends asked pointedly, "Why is your husband that color?" My answer was that we lived in Georgia longer than any other place because we were to be the "enlightened contrast" to the bigots.

Once at a friend's party, the husband began to tell horrible racist jokes, one more egregious than the next. Other guests were embarrassed. I had to leave. The next day I called to tell the wife it was her responsibility to keep control of her party and to stop her husband. I explained that my husband, who she and her spouse professed to love, had some African blood. I told her it was her responsibility as hostess to stop her husband, and that if it ever happened again in my presence, that I would stop him. Proof of the enduring nature of true friendship is that the wife and I are still friends today.

I consider it a God-given gift that when I've had to call friends on their misbehavior or mistaken beliefs not backed up by the facts that they have wanted to remain friends with me. Having been a teacher of wine-drinking adults for decades without anyone ever being guilty of DUI (driving under the influence), I have earned a voice of authority—moral authority—or no one would have paid $350 per person to hear what I had to say in a wine course.

18

WRITER, FIGHTER...TEACHER

TEACHERS HAVE TO be in control of the class, no matter how hard it is sometimes. I only had to assert my authority a couple times in thousands of classes, and both those times were when the class was made up of liquor salesmen—or adults who had too many cocktails before class. I threatened to cancel the course because they were ruining it for the other students. And I said no refunds.

Anyone who has ever seen me perform knows I mean what I say and I say what I mean. I could gauge the mood of the audience, figure out what funny line would grab their attention, cram a boat load of knowledge into them, inspire them and perform like a somewhat X-rated stand-up comedian to make the otherwise very technical and potentially boring subject of wine fascinating, and then finally sing for them. They would reward me with such love and good feeling that I'd be on a "high" for hours after, though I was and had to be the sober one.

Most important, I got used to being stared at by audiences when I was the "dolly with the hole in her stocking." I was once asked to sing a cappella 3 verses of "America, the Beautiful" for hundreds of Military in Tampa for a culinary awards weekend. My knees were knocking, but I got a standing ovation. That took guts, but no guts, no glory.

A roommate in London said my tombstone epitaph should read, "Anita was a writer and a fighter." My inclination is to fight, even if it costs me and even if no one else involved wants to. But I do so first with my mind, second with my voice, and third I put pen to paper. My pen has a sharp point.

Like the very prolific best-selling author, James Patterson, I write "cursive" or longhand, which research has shown stimulates our more creative right brain. Children who are not taught cursive handwriting in school miss getting this easy access to their higher mind. The creative process of my free verse poems may take weeks of thinking as I formulate the theme, but once I begin writing, it takes only 10 minutes per poem. Then I rush to type it in the computer and find that it needs almost no editing. I know it's good when other people tell me it moved them.

I've often said that I can add $2 + 2 = 6$ instead of 4. My husband would corroborate this—but then why wouldn't he believe me from the outset? A prophet is seldom given credit in their own time. When I arrived in Atlanta from

London, I raved about Australia wines and told the wine wholesalers they needed to represent and distribute them. I knew about Australia wines because the wine store where I worked in London was down the street from the Australian Wine Centre. The Atlanta wine wholesalers and importers said, "Kangaroo wines, Anita, do you think we're crazy?" I replied, "I do now!" Needless to say, these same wholesalers have made millions of dollars selling Australian wines since then.

19

SHORTCOMING

My ADMITTED SHORTCOMING was one many women share, i.e., when I so impressed the bosses that they asked me what I wanted (in addition to the money they were paying me), I didn't ask for more! How I regret that I didn't speak up to the owner of one very large wholesaler who was a philanthropist in the community and ask him for what I really wanted at that time—a wine center.

Lesson to be learned by the teacher, as I allude to in my poem "100 Million Votes"—women must do what men are quick to do, ask or you won't get! The consequences will be that you'll end up having to beg for what you've earned. There is no next time—the time is *now*.

Male colleagues in Atlanta were already so jealous of this young female upstart that they bad-mouthed me at every turn when they had never seen me perform in front of a class or wine event audience. So it was by my own design that I did not tell them I had as many as 82 people in a class, or that readers of my monthly wine columns in magazines, or people worldwide who e-mailed me wine questions when I was an online wine expert for CNN.com, would write such glowing evaluations of my work. Quite often, I stuck these in a file cabinet without reading them until I had a bad day and then would rediscover them as I was clearing papers. My advice to other women is to keep a low profile but document your work product—make a video of your reports—then e-mail it to coworkers.

And the best advice I can give anyone about getting the most from your job or giving the most to your employees--even if you're a small business--is to put your earnings into savings! Employers can set up a free retirement plan with the U.S. Treasury at MyRA.gov Or try HonestDollar.com or ForUsAll.com for other 401(k)s. Self-employed workers have several options too for savings through large investment companies.

You become a legend when other people say you are one. I have been so lucky to have been praised for my charisma, teaching abilities, and as a catalyst for changing lives for the better. Twenty years after people graduated from my classes, they were still phoning me to say thank you and that they were still toasting my health. I said, "That's probably the only reason I'm still standing!" A teacher teaches like a writer writes or a performer performs—because they have to. Something inside assures me all three of the hats I wear are what I've always been meant to do—my mission. And I've felt on the hook to God since the beginning.

20

VALEDICTORIAN

How BRAVE I was then, actually using the n-word to illustrate there was no excuse ever to denigrate another human being, even an anti-Semite word to speak against fascism and hatred of the Jews, or misogynistic words that belittled me and my entire gender.

We all wish we had the energy and fervor of our youth when we felt the world was at our feet and we were in our element of newness. Every day I try to recapture that bold spirit. The old Latin saying "Fortune favors the bold" is really "Fortune favors the brave" as it is the fearlessness of youth we must hold in our hearts, minds, and bodies as we get older. Aging is inevitable, part of being human, but our spirit doesn't diminish. It lights our eyes even as our sight dims. Many of the most accomplished people, past and present, received their greatest awards late in life. Americans in particular can expect to have more than 2 or 3 careers or changes of direction in their lives. Standing still is stagnation, and we all know how the scum builds up in standing water.

"Going with the flow" was considered "new age" crap by many who abhorred the youth culture of the '60s. But flowing water is exactly what you need to be so that the buildup of toxic situations and people don't clog your drains and dreams.

If our Military's Joint Chiefs were to ask me how to get rid of the bad apples, I'd respond like a housewife and tell them to "pour on the Drano and flush that clog right out of the system."

This may be particularly relevant regarding "drug (and alcohol) rehab," which I am told is now done right on Army bases for soldiers with these addiction problems.

We have a responsibility to see that our soldiers and veterans at VA hospitals get the help they need to overcome these addictions or problems with painkillers etc. Obamacare also has provisions for rehab.

21

KARMA CATCH-UP

My 11th LEVEL of hell—worse than Dante's 9th level of sinners who fail to take action in a moral crisis, or Jodi Picoult's *10th level* in her book of the same name, which is where people who lie to themselves end up—would be reserved for those who would dare to make others doubt themselves. By killing another person's dreams for themselves, we divert them from their spiritual path and stop them from fulfilling their destiny.

If you are guilty of belittling those closest to you, stop. When you prevent other people from loving themselves, you cannot expect them or anyone else to love you in return.

Karma catch-up, I call it. Whenever we do wrong to others, karma will do to you what you've done to them. Otherwise savvy con men are always surprised when they get caught. Why be surprised when you play the angles and percentages and know the "house always wins" in casinos as in life? Very disingenuous of you, masters of the universe types, not to expect be hung by your own tie.

Criminals could save the world in no time if they would apply their considerable brain power to our dilemmas. Instead, they are always on the make, always on the take. Why? Because they know they are imposters and unworthy of our society. So they segregate themselves in gated enclaves lest the masses be allowed in.

We in the other 99 percent can out vote them, but unfortunately, we have a very low voter turnout rate compared to countries such as India, which had 150 million voters cast ballots in the last national election. India also had one of the first and most effective women prime ministers—Indira Ghandi. And after years of house arrest by the ruling military junta, Nobel Peace Prize winner Aung San Suu Kyi won national elections and has become the defacto president of her country Burma/Myanmar. The superpower U.S. was until now a long way from electing our first woman president and vice president despite TV series showing women in the White House doing a fantastic, but pretend, job of representing our interests here at home and worldwide.

Like the ant trying to move the rubber tree plant in the song made famous by Frank Sinatra, I have high hopes we will have our first woman president by the 100th anniversary of women's suffrage (women getting the vote). Please refer to my poem "100 Million Votes" performed by me as the last of *3 Valentine's Day Poems* on YouTube.com to catch the fervor.

How can women be taken seriously until they occupy the halls of power equally with men? My poem asks men to show us their respect for the breath of life we gave them and belief we are their equals by voting for a woman president. What may be the greatest obstacle are women who fear their power, who run from it instead of running with the wolves. Find the goddess within you, and be warrior angels for our cause. It's your cause too. Show your female credentials with pride. Don't deny other women what you take for yourselves.

22

SOMETHING MORE

IN MY FREE verse poem "Mirror Image & Something More," I say men cannot be a god without a goddess. And I say that men are wasting their valuable time in defiance and denial. My challenge to men is countered by my challenge to women who must live up to their highest calling.

Women friends I've known and loved for decades sometimes feel little empathy for other women. They blame the victims of sexual assault and say women shouldn't even be in the Military or at the Military Academies because they're putting themselves on the firing line and can expect to be assaulted.

But does our Military ever need them! Every man who signs up in the Military swears to protect and defend our Constitution which ensures life, liberty, and the pursuit of happiness to all our citizens, more than half of which are women.

The U.S. Military has been very good at advancing African American soldiers to the rank of 3 & 4 Star Generals. They are the best of the best. Although 35 percent of Military women are minorities, they have not been given the same assist to advancement. If the color of their skin or ethnicity is not holding them back, then it must be the fact that they are women. Our Military needs to be as gender-blind as it is color-blind.

As we were about to print my book, Secretary of Defense Ash Carter announced March 19, 2016 that 4-Star Air Force General Lori Robinson will become the first woman combat commander and most senior woman in U.S. Military history as head of USNORTHCOM with responsibility for the defense of the U.S., Canada & Mexico in case of enemy attack. We'll be in good hands under her guard. And now I'm an even bigger fan of Secretary Carter's.

23

DIPLOMACY

DIPLOMACY DOES NOT mean bending to the whims of every rogue in power. There is no dealing with madmen, even when they are leading strategic countries. But effective Military strategy applies here, and it may be possible to beat them at their own irrational games.

Economic sanctions do work, especially when people have a good reason to apply emotion when they take out their wallets. Yes, we feel for the poor people of Russia who depend on exports to the U.S. for their livelihood. But then let them put pressure on their supposedly elected leaders to actually lead them to prosperity for all.

Amazing how the destitute could become the most enterprising of entrepreneurs if there was truly a free market in their country. It's in our human nature to strive to better ourselves. But there is no physical energy to strive on empty stomachs growling with hunger. This is particularly true in dictatorships such as North Korea and Syria.

Maybe we need to focus on feeding our own starving in the U.S. first and foremost. But too often our foreign policy is grossly over budget. Make it cost effective for us. Challenge other countries to pay their fair share for American goods and expertise. Don't give it away. Congress is now requiring countries who receive U.S. financial aid to improve the status of women in their countries as part of the renewal of the Violence Against Women Act.

24

OUR WORLD

Let's step up to the plate as world leaders in this area and make clever use of our resources. And one of our greatest resources is women. If we do have a day of rest for women and girls in the U.S. the day after our 2016 presidential election, then I call on every well-established corporate or businesswoman to open up their office buildings to women on that day for self-empowerment seminars.

Women attorneys can offer free legal advice, women doctors can volunteer at women's health clinics, and women parishioners, park officials, and librarians can make sure churches, parks, and libraries are open to women who need sanctuary or downtime in nature.

Men will claim that if women and girls do this that we'll wreck the economy, but I didn't say we wouldn't spend money on our day of rest—we'll just spend it on ourselves Our economic power will demonstrate once and for all how valuable women are to society. And the girls come with us, so they can learn from women about life, love, and work. By the way, gays of either gender or transgender people are welcome to join us. We don't judge—we are your mothers and sisters who love you unconditionally. One former grade school teacher said, "The schools would close!"—and the hospitals without female nurses—if women took the day off. I responded, "Let the men teach their sons to respect women and not to abuse them. Let the men take care of their sons at home, or by taking them to work. Let the men multitask as women do every day!"

What is the definition of "feminist"? It is standing up for equality, for equal treatment under the law, for equal rights for all women. The U.S. never passed the Equal Rights Amendment to our Constitution because the men in power in each of the states refused to grant women what they had granted all men, even black men. And men want to show their displeasure and resentment that women want the same advantages in 2016? Real men are not threatened, but rather act as secret feminists to help their own daughters, wives, sisters. Too bad it has to be a secret. At the 2016 World Economic Forum's annual meeting, Canada's Prime Minister Justin Trudeau was quoted as saying he was a feminist, and that: "We shouldn't be afraid of the word feminist. Men & women should use it to describe themselves." He also declared that he will raise his sons to be feminists. I only hope my book will encourage other men to say "I am a feminist".

25

REALITY CHECK

REALITY CHECK, MEN—IF you want to dance at home, then let us dance in the streets. While you're at it, men, be sure to clean at least one main room in the house and have dinner ready for your wives and sweethearts and daughters at the end of our day of rest. Show good faith, men, and as I say in my poem, you'll be heroes of a happy home. Bet you'll be praying we never do this again! The truth that you'll never admit to is you really can't live without us. Because then you'd be alone with yourselves.

But I've observed that men (including my dear departed husband) need distraction from the fact that they are unwilling to share substantive emotional thoughts with other men. Women do so easily and are the most emotionally supportive of each other and men. Men are too critical and judgmental to ever help women resolve a crisis. Remember that, ladies! So, men, if you need group therapy, always make sure women are participating. And for this, we get no respect. The truth is men are the babies who never grow up.

And do not say I am a "ball buster"—I've given men back their manhood all my life. And I'm not a dominatrix either—I'm not into pain, mine or anybody else's. Remember, I said Venus is my ruler. I love men and obviously would never choose to live without them. But I require a man, a real man who can take a woman with finesse, not force. You give nothing, you get nothing. If you only want a one-night stand—or less than one-night stand, meaning it's all over in the first half-hour—then the only women who'll take you up on it will be: 1. Women who are not as highly evolved; 2. Women who want to treat you like a boy toy; 3. Women who are not in control of their stick; 4. Women who are married or trying to bring you into a triangle; and 5. Women who are a "fatal attraction" and will victimize you!

Any decent woman would say "No, thanks" to your indecent proposal, but if they make the mistake of saying yes, they'll feel terrible afterward and never want to see you again. End result: you won't get much practice making love.

26

DIVINE MIND

IT'S THE SMART man who would ask his lover what they want most of all. For me it's "mutual surrender." That means we acknowledge we're equally strong in different ways and each bring much to the relationship. To make any romantic relationship work requires the respect accorded Generals who are generous in victory and gracious in defeat. That's how to avoid battles and get to the bedroom.

As I write this at speed—500 words every 15 minutes, 2,000 words longhand per hour—in one of Tom Bird's "write your book in a weekend retreats" (go to TomBird. com for all the details and free downloads of his books), I am most intrigued by the very youngest member of our group, a 21-year-old guy from Orlando who is working as an office administrator right out of high school.

He read that one has to write a million words before they're ever good enough to be published. Well, I have written 3 wine books and published hundreds of magazine articles on the subject of wine. All of which earned me a paycheck—and now I have the discipline to be creative and cover the meaning of metaphysics and human geography on less than a page in a free verse poem. This impressed young Orlando. I was impressed by him and the other 27 writers in our group, who insisted that I use my life as the template for this book on problem solving. They were also adamant that I include sex and romance in this book, and Tom Bird told me, "You have an explosive personality, Anita, and I expect an explosive book from you." Thanks to all of you for helping me birth this book.

One of the woman writers, Nancy Forbes, at Tom Bird's retreat had been in my Wine School years before with her husband who joined us so we could get re-acquainted. Also in 2015, I met a woman at a party who had been in my Oglethorpe University wine class years ago. And at a wine dinner at a well-known Italian restaurant, the woman sitting across from me had bought my wine book and recognized me. I love and thank all my wine graduates for remembering.

P.S. Once I'd written 30,000 words longhand, life and editing intervened. It took 2 months to get the publishing contract, another month to interview the Colonels, and then every week after that brought new headlines and updates of the Military content. Typing it all and refining the wording were hard.

And then I bought a wonderful new hardcover book from one of my earliest mentors, a man who is certainly one of the greatest California winemakers: Richard G. Peterson's *The Winemaker* was published September 2015 and is available for $34.95 from RichardGPeterson.com. He's had a fascinating life—from Iowa farm boy, to Marine in Korea, graduate education on the GI Bill, and a stellar career making great wines for many vineyards and now his own Napa winery Richard Grant. The reason I mention Dr. Peterson is that he used a photo of himself at age 17 on the cover of his book—and that has inspired me to include here an age progression of photographs from babyhood to high school, Cornell to London, & Atlanta. Dr. Peterson is in one of the photos I've included.

When I reconnected with a woman friend from Cornell—Millie Tripp—this many years later she said I looked the same in my Facebook photo, only older. I wish. We all lose our charms in the end. But red wine is a preservative!

27

PARADE YOUR PERSONALITY

ALWAYS BE TRUE to yourselves and your vision. Don't let anyone rain on your parade or rain on anyone else's parade. But make sure it is a fun parade with marching band and cheerleaders. It's the only way to go.

At times I was told I was too loud, too brash—until the next group said I was Ms. Personality and had charisma to spare and was unforgettable. Audiences I discovered were attracted to my passion. Let's hope the magic happens on these pages as well. I've pulled the pin on this hand grenade.

Ah, the years it has taken to become such a magician. You cannot write what you haven't lived. In order to have something to say, you must have firsthand experience of the joys and heartaches of living. And you must have pushed to your very limits or you won't have the confidence to stand totally honest and revealed in front of an audience. It was me in the world all by myself, and there is little I fear now.

People sense that personal power, and if they are insecure, they are so threatened by it that they will attack me verbally without me even having addressed them. Have I ever hit back? Never—truly strong people do not need to prove themselves by hurting weaker or innocent people. There is a great difference between having a strong personality and being an abuser. Abusers were often abused themselves. I'm definitely an "intimidator" personality type, secure in myself and able to help myself as well as everyone else. And yeah, I'm a girl. I asked my sister Diana, "Have I ever knowingly hurt anyone in my life?" She said no. Of that, I am most proud.

But God save me from the "poor me" personality types! In James Redfield's groundbreaking book *The Celestine Prophecy*, he enumerates the four basic personality types: Intimidators who are so honest that other people can't take it! What you see is what you get—a no hidden agenda, direct, assertive, compulsive leader, organizer, or manager who can always take care of themselves but still be emotionally vulnerable like me.

Unfortunately, Intimidator personality types attract the Poor-Me types who look for someone to take care of them. They blame the world for their woes but are quick to expect and accept the world's help. Once Intimidators realize they've taken on the Poor-Me's karma, which is wrong—they stop laying the golden eggs, and the Poor-Me types become resentful and passive-aggressive.

Intimidators don't even understand the word *passive*, especially when attached to aggressive, which they do understand. Poor-Mes promise to do something or be somewhere and don't. It's their way of getting back at the Intimidators, or anyone who wants to force them to stand on their own two feet. Many Poor-Mes are depressed, and their depression can be very self-centered.

The other two personality types also have a fatal attraction for each other: The Secret Agent types (Redfield calls them aloof types) and the Interrogators. The Secret Agent types never want you to know what they really think, or feel, what they do or have done. This means they lie to themselves (10th level of hell) and act contrary to their own hearts and best interests in their efforts to lie to others and blend in.

Interrogator personality types love asking Secret Agent types: "What are you thinking right now? What did you do today? How do you really feel about us?" This constant barrage of questions drives the Secret Agent (think James Bond character) crazy.

That money lesson Dad taught me at age 7 set my understanding for life. I have an appreciation for money, and hard work, and what it means to pay off debts. But money has never ruled me. It is not my sole motivation. Not as important as a clear conscience and knowing I've never betrayed family to get it.

The significance of my Dad's choice of house on our street did not come out until I read about the Rosicrucians years later. My Dad must have been one because he insisted on buying this particular house because our front door faced a Lutheran church across a barely two-lane blacktop road. And that church door had a large wood cross on it, while above it rose a majestic steeple topped by another more monumental cross. And my Dad was the one who planted those double-sized white roses down the right side of our house.

My Dad was very into "mind power," and that's what Rosicrucians are—individuals (they are not a cult) who self-study the power of the mind, and their symbol is the cross of Christ with a white rose at its center. Though he never went to mass with us on Sunday, he was a believer and insisted on last rites, including last confession, and a full mass funeral. He knew my mother was a saint for putting up with him and that their constant fighting did not mean they didn't love each other. He wanted to be waiting for her in Heaven—she died five years later on the anniversary of his death.

28

LIFE OF PI

THE 2012 MOVIE *Life of Pi*, based on Yann Martel's very spiritual book, is an allegory for life itself. The story illustrates that life is facing down a live tiger every day who wants to eat you as you float helplessly on the open ocean in a life boat for 245 days waiting for rescue. It was nominated for an Academy award.

A beautiful film, narrated by the Indian boy who survived and grew to manhood, it has deep meaning in the moral of the story. The moral of the story is that in order to survive life, we must believe in something greater than ourselves, i.e., a higher power. Doesn't matter what religion—the hero was born a Hindu in India but also studied Buddhism and was a fan of Jesus Christ—but you won't survive without faith in the divine.

That's what gave the young Indian boy the hope and will to live. That and the animal training his zookeeper father taught him, i.e., you can't be friends with a wild animal, but you can train them not to eat you, at least for a time. The boy's name Pi was short for Piscine, French for swimming pool. His uncle taught him to swim underwater, which saved the boy from drowning and the abbreviated nickname stuck because the boy could fill a blackboard with digits of the mathematical symbol pi after the decimal point.

The story resonated with me because I lived my own *Life of Pi* facing down my year-of-the-tiger Dad every day of my life from birth to age 18 when I left home for college. My faith has sustained me throughout, and without it, I would not have had any hope of survival. I highly recommend everyone rent this movie.

Which brings me to the most disturbing documentary I watched on PBS at the end of November 2015—*India's Daughter*—which can be seen on YouTube.com. It is about the brutal gang rape of a 23-year-old female medical student in Delhi who died two weeks later from massive internal injuries. The British filmmaker Leslee Udwin clearly shows that this horrific, but all-too-common crime in India was due to corrosive social and cultural attitudes toward women.

The six gang rapists who are now in jail had been drinking, and said the young woman needed to be punished because she went to see the movie *Life of Pi* to celebrate the completion of her medical studies with a male friend, and should not have been out at 8:30 PM. The rapists drove what looked like a public bus around the city at night many times before to entrap innocent women to rape them on the bus, as they did with this young woman. They even beat her male companion and threw him naked from the bus along with her. Their defense attorneys said the woman should have expected to be treated like this.

This rape was so horrible that it led to widespread protests in the streets of Delhi for a month—and most of the protestors were men—male students who defied police! It also led to changes in criminal laws regarding rape. The filmmaker started the Equality Studies Global Initiative to teach empathy, respect, and the valuing of women and girls. The statistics at the end of the film were shocking: "Globally 1 in 3 women are raped—a percentage that is the same in developed countries such as Australia or England, as it is in developing or undeveloped countries." It listed 17.7 million American women and girls as having been raped since records were kept. Now can you understand why my plea for men to become better men, and for our culture to change its attitude toward women, is so very strong in this book?

29

DOMESTIC VIOLENCE

EVERY NINE SECONDS in the U.S. a woman is assaulted or beaten. Domestic violence is the leading cause of injury to women—more than car accidents, muggings, and rapes combined. Studies suggest up to ten million children witness some form of domestic violence annually. Men who were child witnesses were twice as likely to abuse their own wives than sons of nonviolent parents.

Every day in the U.S. women are murdered by their husbands and boyfriends. Domestic violence and emotional abuse are behaviors used by one person in a relationship to control the other person. Married or nonmarried partners, heterosexual or homosexual, are included in the statistics.

Barbara Corcoran, the very successful New York Real Estate businesswoman on *Shark Tank* very humorously said, "First men 'dis' [disrespect] you then they want to kiss you." If this is your story, leave! Get help before it turns to domestic violence. The National Domestic Violence

Hotline website is TheHotLine.org. Also the Domestic Violence website that includes information on women's shelters, attorneys who specialize in domestic violence, and the laws in different states is DomesticViolence.org. Other very useful Web sites are DomesticViolenceLaws.com, and Laws.com/domesticviolence.

As I mentioned briefly in an earlier chapter the new website NoMore.org sponsored by Avon Foundation, the National Alliance to end Sexual Violence, Kaiser Permanente and many corporations such as Macy's, Allstate, Verizon etc. and the NFL has loads of useful information to help prevent Domestic Violence. We cannot be bystanders. There will be a "No More Week" March 6-12 sponsored by Mary Kay, and we all need to participate by signing up, buying No More charitable products and learning how to respond. Get help here for yourself or for others.

While we are on this subject, help for the "one in four" college women who have survived rape or attempted rape can be found at website OneInFourUSA.org. We can change for the better, and men can help. Men who volunteered to enter men's programs were helped to understand how women can recover from rape, how to increase the likelihood of intervention in a potentially high-risk situation, and how to change their own behaviors and influence the behavior of other men.

Women's programs can help them recognize high-risk predators, can empower them to intervene on behalf of other women in high-risk situations, and give pertinent information about rape, recovery, and resources.

Researchers estimate that one in six men also experience abusive sexual relationships before the age of consent. The website 1in6.com helps men who've had unwanted or abusive sexual experience in childhood live healthier, happier lives. Reason enough for me to spend so much time on male sexual assault in previous chapters.

My poem "Fifty Shades—Envisage Nothing" that follows is, I hope, a slap across the face of predators who deserve it. I challenge the author of the mega-best selling but very repetitive book to donate some of her ill-gotten gains to appropriate domestic violence charities—for Queen and country because the author is British. Queen Elizabeth II and Britain's foreign minister have hosted a worldwide symposium on violence against women in London that was attended by representatives from many countries including Angelina Jolie Pitt from the U.S.

The movie version of this book, *Fifty Shades of Grey*, scored a huge number of tickets sold in the U.S., but movie reviewers unanimously panned it with an average rating of D for making even kinky sex boring. Though young American women came out in droves to see a college age virgin be abused in the "red room" of some fictional billionaire sadist, young men in the audience were thoroughly confused because every time he hurt the young woman, he bought her off with a new car or private airplane ride to some exotic destination. Please do not give young men mixed messages that it's okay to abuse your wife or girlfriend, or boyfriend, as long as you give them money. That's prostitution.

Read for yourself whether I've come on too strong. I've always wondered why some woman attorney like Gloria Allred in Los Angeles doesn't try to sue the author of the *Fifty Shades* trilogy under our U.S. Violence Against Women Act.

FIFTY SHADES & ENVISAGE NOTHING

Predator or prey is the only choice you offer. Is it any wonder a Hollywood star backed out of playing your hero?

He is neither Christian, nor grey, but rather predominantly and contractually black as mortal sin—and a criminal, even if the virgin signs.

May every titillated young girl or woman who reads this rubbish wise up! Sick men need no additional excuses for hurting you.

Rape is not sexy. Ask the 3 kidnapped and imprisoned young women who escaped from that vile, but so ordinary, man's house of shame—or the many unknown girls murdered worldwide dumped like trash by their killers.

I'm a former Londoner, but Mrs. British housewife "E. L. James," your writing is as false as your name and has no redeeming value whatsoever. Your trilogy incites abuse of women.

Right your wrong, and spend the foolish millions you've made on appropriate domestic violence charities—for Queen & country.

30

CHURCHES

ONE OF MY favorite *Doonesbury* cartoons by G. (Gary) B. Trudeau starts out by asking, "Who is this frat boy monster? Who tells his victim that he 'had a great time?' And why do our most trusted institutions—universities, the church, the Military—continue to cover up sexual violence crimes that in any other context would result in long prison terms!"

Although I've been a journalist I forgot who first broke the story about pedophile Catholic priests until I saw the recent hit movie "Spotlight" which chronicled the Boston Globe's investigative reporters who wrote 600 articles covering over 1,000 victims of the 249 Boston priests whose cases of sexual molestation of children had to be settled by the Catholic Church. At the end of the movie there was a huge list of cities with priest scandals all over the world. A psychologist in the movie who had treated these priests said 50% of priests are not celibate and fully 6% are pedophiles. Spotlight won the Oscar for Best Picture at the Academy

Awards, February 28, 2016, and the producers ended their acceptance speech with the Catholic Church must finally deal with this problem. Since then, Palm Sunday 2016, the Catholic Church's Sunday Visitor openly detailed the story of Johnstown, PA's 50 pedophile priests.

I'm not the only one who is drawing a parallel between the U.S. Military and the Catholic Church. The Military must open to women soldiers and sailors, and the Catholic Church must allow qualified women to enter the seminaries. We can all understand why celibate clerics in the Catholic Church would have a hard time understanding why their women members are so upset at their chauvinist mentality that is far removed from the reality of independent and educated women in the 21st century who resent continued condescension. Same goes for top Military officers, most of whom are from earlier generations. They just don't get it!

My real estate broker friend, Betty Oliver, told me many churches are in foreclosure and empty and up for sale—of all denominations. She paraphrased the moral teacher, Joyce Meyer, who said, "Sitting in church every week does not make you spiritual or moral, or a Christian! Just as sitting in a garage does not make you a car." People go to church and often act immorally out of church.

My husband and I once attended a weekend of silence at a Jesuit retreat in Atlanta where we each got one-on-one counseling. I will never forget what my Jesuit counselor told me when I couldn't understand why my "born-again

Christian" magazine editor would purposely hold back my monthly topic until three days before every deadline. The Jesuit priest said, "Sometimes self-professed born-again Christians are neither Christian nor born-again." He also told me I was one of the most persevering and follow-through of people he had ever met, because I had never missed a monthly deadline in ten years, in spite of the hindrance.

By the way, the Buddhists may have a better approach and philosophy to sobriety than the classic 12-step model. The Buddhists keep the spirituality but take it in a different direction. Their meditation techniques have proven useful to recovering alcoholics, as has more modern meditation techniques such as "mindfulness meditation." Anderson Cooper reported on "mindfulness" in the CBS program *60 Minutes* that aired September 6, 2015. He discovered that practicing mindfulness reduces stress, improves memory, and helps with chronic pain/illness and addiction. Mindfulness meditation was started by a man called Kabat-Zinn but is also done by many companies including Google, for their staff. Again, we must put our electronic devices down and become aware of our breath and being—especially if we are to be as focused as Special Operations soldiers.

Earlier in my book, I asked, "Where were the MPs?" when wondering about sex trafficking and drug running going on right under their noses. I want to facetiously ask, "Where is Jack Reacher when you need him?" Jack Reacher is the 6'5" former Major and Army MP fictional hero of the Lee Child mysteries. He is a detective who can move his 250-pound, all muscle, body against at least half a dozen men at a time—and put them all in the hospital.

In Lee Child's latest Jack Reacher novel *Make Me*, there is a point where he mentions Pascal's Wager before a shootout with the bad guys. Pascal was a French philosopher/mathematician who lived in the 1600s and argued that all humans bet with their lives either that God exists or that He doesn't. If we assume that the wager is infinite if God exists, then there is at least a small chance that God does in fact exist. Therefore, Pascal argues a reasonable person must live as though God exists and seek to believe in God. If God does not exist, we will have only a limited loss of some pleasures, but we stand to receive infinite gain, such as eternal life in Heaven, and avoid infinite loss, such as ending up in Hell.

Go to Wikipedia for more explanation. The Lee Child book heroes rush in to fight the evildoers figuring if God exists, He'll be on their side. And what crimes were the evildoers committing? They were making "snuff" films "to order" for money of the torture, rape, and murder of innocent people for subscribers on the "deep web."

31

LAST POEM

"Sword Through The Heart" is the poem I wrote just before this book as solace for everyone—including myself as a recent widow—who has ever had a broken heart from the loss of a loved one. Ostensibly, it's about a romantic breakup, which was the outcome of my first grand passion, nearly 4-year affair, at Cornell.

But the poem is really about every kind of lost love, including that of losing a child to suicide. I wrote the poem while staying with a dear woman friend in Bellaire, Florida, who had lost her young son to suicide years earlier when she lived in Atlanta. It moved me to have her say the poem spoke to her too.

What did happen to that first love at Cornell? I got him his dream of Harvard Business School—I got the application, filled it out, wrote the essay, attached his transcripts, got him to sign it, mailed it off, and he got in! How stupid I was then—I really wanted to go myself. In fact, I ended up spending every extra dollar I had while in my first year of my Cornell Master's degree going back and forth to Cambridge visiting him and attending his classes. Couldn't help putting my hand up to answer the MBA professors.

But he cheated on me with a woman who knew he had a girlfriend. Through my copious tears, I actually felt sorry for her because she got a lot more than she bargained for with him. Later he had the gall to tell me he didn't want to marry her but didn't have the guts to tell her no now that he'd said yes. Years later in Atlanta, a fraternity brother of his brought evidence that my lover's bad deeds had not been forgotten and that God arranged for me to know this was his Karma catch-up.

In my poem "Sword Through The Heart," I say there are no innocent bystanders, that friends are obligated to tell other friends not to self-destruct because of someone else's destructiveness. My Master's degree was completed the following year, and a friend from that graduate school period recently faxed me a photo she had kept of us two young women—gorgeous but abandoned by our men—standing in front of the ivy-covered sociology building.

The Cornell man broke my heart, so I went to Europe that summer with some housemates to get away from the pain. Before I left Ithaca, I met my ideal man. He was a karate sensei (Master) with a new studio near campus. Very dark and exotic looking, I recall he had grandparents who were Italian, Jewish, Buddhist, and Muslim, and he was a few years older and had an injured leg—from the Vietnam War I presumed. He certainly moved with the agility of someone who had Special Forces training.

With the kinetic energy of a coiled snake, he flew across the studio floor as he instructed advanced students in mind/body martial arts. I was fascinated and knew he was a master teacher. He took me to dinner, ever the courtly gentleman, on three dates, and for hours afterward, he would sit opposite me on his sofa and just stare into my eyes. Needless to say, by the third date, he had my undivided attention. He hesitated to begin an affair with me because his woman had come back after a 2-year absence. I was sad but very appreciative that he would not betray his woman. Then he proceeded to teach me a master class in myself.

He told me that my motto was "Time and Anita wait for no man." He said I was like time itself—eternal. The gratitude I felt was immeasurable. I was vulnerable, and he could have taken advantage of my emotional fragility. Instead he made me stronger. Control, he had it to the nth degree. Discipline, integrity, ethics, and enough mind power for a Rasputin. But all for good, not evil.

No need to force an issue or another person when you are that sure of who you are. He sent me off to London with more fight in me than I had ever had in a lifetime of skirmishes with opponents. His opinion of me restored my faith in myself and gave me hope that there were good men out there for me to meet.

Girlfriends had told me, look for a male Anita LaRaia. I never found him, someone who would be a life, love, and work partner. But did meet my twin that summer in Europe—a Swede who was just as tall, just as blonde, just as blue-eyed and just as handsome as my lost love and a whole lot nicer. He became only the second man of three men I had ever loved. The third was my husband.

Oh, yes, I had many men in London as my poem "Drive" alludes to, but I was never in the backseat of any car with a testosterone-fueled high school boy. Had to make the poem funny and sexy so men would get the moral of the story.

The moral of the poem "Drive" was that men need to keep control of their sticks and need to choose a woman who's in control of hers. That way, both avoid road blocks and dead ends as they try to cruise to ecstasy.

I know most young guys go out of their way to make a woman lose control by plying her with large quantities of alcohol, but that's not the way to true love that lasts. Common sense would tell you that. Trust is essential in any relationship destined to stand the test of time.

Dame Judy Dench voiced one of my all-time favorite lines of movie dialogue in one of the James Bond films in her role as "M," head of MI5, the British spy agency. A General in their war room looks down his nose at her and asks how can a woman be head of MI5? She replies in perfect deadpan, "At least I don't ever have to think with that appendage dangling between your legs."

It is a handicap we don't have as women, thank God. As for the interbranch rivalry among Military men, it's as if they're always comparing dicks. I call it "saber rattling" with their other "sabers."

32

THE LUCK FACTOR

THE LUCK FACTOR book prompted me to start keeping an intuition journal, a record of specific incidents where my intuition saved the day. I had already been keeping a daily diary of all my activities and a dream diary as well. It is so natural for a writer to write. I even filled an entire blank journal my sister had given me with letters to her about happenings in her life over a three-year period. She cried when she received that journal Christmas gift back from me.

People always assume that because I talk a lot that I'm not listening, but I can repeat back to them details of their lives that they told me years before. I do listen, especially now as we are all getting older and our time together may be limited.

Returning to the subject of luck, *The Luck Factor* studies demonstrate and confirm we make our own luck. Lucky people seize opportunities others never even see. Lucky people, like myself, have lots of practice taking sour lemons and making splendid lemonade. My intuition journal filled a notebook with incidents such as the time my husband drove our car even though it was making very disturbing engine sounds. I insisted we stop at a local restaurant for lunch so I could think. Then I insisted we drive to the car repair service on the other side of that parking lot. My husband wanted to go home. I said *no*. The mechanics said if he had driven one more mile, he would have burned out his engine and would have cost us thousands of dollars to replace it.

It has also been very useful for connecting with my Divine mind to keep a dream diary since 1984. Often our dreams are just a result of anxiety, but sometimes they are uplifting and even prophetic. That's why I record the most vivid ones which usually come about 7-8 AM. I've trained myself to wake up and write these dreams down on paper. Also, to really plug into your true intuition, you must stop, sit or lie down, and clear your mind to allow the answer to appear in it.

I'm also exceptionally good at using my intuition to find lost objects—once an antique gold and pearl ring that had fallen off my finger when I was disposing of kitty litter that I found in the garbage can outside just in time before garbage pick-up, and another time when my husband panicked because he lost an expensive gold and jade ring I had bought him in Hawaii that he thought he had left in a restaurant men's room. After two trips back to the restaurant in spite of the fact I told him my intuition said the ring had not been lost there, he finally found the ring inside his shorts where it had fallen when he used the urinal. He was so relieved, he didn't mind when I rocked with laughter.

Men who've read my poem "Jeweled Butterfly" wrote me that they only hope someone would love them that much to write such a beautiful poem when they return to the stars.

33

WORK IS MORE THAN A JOB

WHEN MY NIECE and nephew were in high school, they'd call me to ask if they should go to college because their parents had not. I said, "Of course, you want good jobs and pay, don't you? And how else are you going to get that in your small town?" I was such a proud auntie when they both went to college.

Now my niece is a well-paid high school physics teacher married to another high school physics teacher she met in college. They have a wonderful son who was the first baby born into our small family in 26 years. My nephew received a Master's degree in college administration, worked at Syracuse University for six years, has now received a promotion to director of admissions at a Texas university, and he's newly married to the love of his life.

Before the recession, it was easier to escape monster bosses by getting another job. As I recommended earlier in my book, Robert I. Sutton's best-seller *The No Asshole Rule* has tips in his chapter 5 that include developing emotional detachment, looking for small wins, building pockets of supportive coworkers, etc. I'd add four more tips: 1) Use your webcam to document everything you create at work with a video then e-mail it to the boss, other execs. Now you have time- and date-stamped evidence. Caution: Do not post this online! Your work product belongs to the company that pays you. 2) Protect yourself before performance reviews by giving your boss a diary of achievements. 3) If you still get bad reviews, defend yourself in a letter with facts for HR to put in your personnel file. 4) Learn to be appropriately funny—no off-color jokes. Positive humor can defeat the black magic of any monster boss and get everyone else on your side.

Progress toward equal pay for woman continues to be made. The year 2015 saw the passage of the California Equal Pay Act, which was signed into law by Governor Jerry Brown. It beefs up the California Labor Code and makes equal pay mandatory with few exceptions, and it allows for lawsuits and money damages. We also have Senator Elizabeth Warren (D-Massachusetts) to thank for our Consumer Financial Protection Bureau and for being money crusader for us all. She is currently working to stop kickbacks on retirees' annuities and to get cost of living raises for Social Security and veterans, and easing student loan debt.

SWORD THROUGH THE HEART

When romantic love ends badly, it can be so hurtful that we wish our barely beating heart would turn to stone.

Lovers put a sword through our hearts because they know we can better handle the pain of a breakup. Their weakness is cruelty to the strong. But the strong will forgive.

No one has the right to make another person doubt themselves or divert them from their spiritual path. It is perhaps the greatest sin, worse than failing to take action in a moral crisis which was Dante's 9th and lowest level of hell.

Trickling blood, your hope is to find a soul mate who can pull the sword from your heart with as much magic as King Arthur who removed Excalibur from the rock.

Opening the wound is the only way to finally heal it. Loving again takes the courage of legend but makes us whole and enables us to feel sympathy and empathy for all suffering.

There are no innocent bystanders. If you truly are a friend of the lovelorn or lost, you will advise them, early and often, from the right side of Heaven not to self-destruct because of someone else's destructiveness.

Out of disaster comes destiny. Forced to become a wizard, you will learn to take sour lemons and make splendid lemonade with no regrets for having loved. Then every crisis or crossroads in life becomes the opportunity you've been waiting for to show proof of your personal power and victory.

34

MEN ARE FROM VENUS, WOMEN ARE FROM MARS

THE BEST-SELLING BOOK by John Gray titled *Men Are from Mars, Women Are from Venus* is often turned upside down in today's battle of the sexes. Men can be stay-at-home Dads, caregivers, and work in what were traditionally women's jobs. While it can be women who go to war, earn more income, or own the family business. This is not just anecdotal, our U.S. economy is based on small businesses, and the great majority of those are run by women. Though family men say they do an equal amount of child-rearing or housework as their mostly full-time working wives, it is still the wives who bear responsibility for seeing that it all gets done.

For years I've said this "superwoman" requirement is ridiculous. My husband and I didn't have children, but he was often completely oblivious to the fact that I wrote every card, bought every gift, remembered every occasion, made every Holiday special, and planned every vacation and our social lives for our family and friends. He worked hard for 8 hours daily, 5 days per week, and I literally did all that plus work nights teaching, weekends doing wine parties, cooked for him every night, and made him happy. Sometimes he would say I was the only thing keeping him alive. I created a good *life* for us—that's what women do.

A few years ago, a government study said the work women do in the home is worth over $600,000 in annual salary when compared to the management skills required. And yet, we get no respect. Another study result, it costs $250,000 per child to raise them from birth to age 18—so that doesn't even include college. The Great Recession brought this brutal reality home for many couples. Child-rearing as well as marriage and living independently from Mom and Dad got postponed, and unplanned pregnancies are down.

It took the women's movement of the 1960s to finally get laws passed to allow single women to get birth control—you had to be married to get the "pill" when I went to Cornell, even if you were 21. And here we are over 50 years later still fighting for this right versus old white men in positions of power who want to curtail access to contraception. But now it appears we've come to our senses—PlanBOneStep.com—the nonprescription "morning after pill" is now available.

35

FULL CIRCLE

I HAD A dream about the radius of a circle—if it was extended to infinity, the diameter, area, and circumference of the circle also expanded. It was all about making the pie unlimited in size so that everyone gets a share.

But that is not possible with our most precious resource—water. I've come full circle back to drinking. One of the most important TV shows I watched this past summer was on PBS—*Climate Change: Global Reality*, hosted by John King. By 2050, our demand for water will increase 55 percent. Yet we waste 30 percent of residential water irrigating our lawns. California grows over half our food in the U.S., and we would need to increase production 70 percent to meet our food needs in the next decade. Yet there simply is not enough water or energy available to do this.

Climate change is economic impact, no matter what the cause. In 2014, the U.S. had 8 natural disasters that cost our economy over $1 billion each. Hurricane Katrina cost us $151 billion, Superstorm Sandy cost $67 billion. 40 percent of the small businesses that closed because of these natural disasters never reopened. It is crucial for our survival to conserve water, even though it may appear we have too much water during severe flooding. It was always erroneous to call it "global warming"—it's climate change, extremes of climate that we cannot deal with. We humans need water. I can give up drinking wine, but not water.

Google "Skoll Initiative" for one of Warren Buffet's Giving Pledge billionaires who lists the five greatest dangers to humanity's survival--and the first two are the most critical Climate Change and Water Security.

The same week I lovingly placed my husband's ashes at sea as per his wishes, I picked up a little book by J. K. Rowling of Harry Potter fame called *Very Good Lives: The Fringe Benefits of Failure and the Importance of Imagination*. It was her commencement address to Harvard University in 2008. From her firsthand knowledge of poverty, she said it entails fear, stress, and depression—it means a thousand petty humiliations and hardship. Talent and intelligence never inoculated anyone against the caprice of the fates, she explained, and I couldn't agree more. But failure gave her inner security because she survived and discovered herself. Imagination, she said, transforms us and enables us to empathize with humans whose experiences we've never shared. For me too, expressive writing heals me and becomes a tool to heal others.

My earliest memory: I am lying in the grass of our front yard at age 5 looking up at the sky and feel the earth revolving under my body. I am a tiny speck on this huge ball of the globe, and yet I am not afraid. I feel the earth's energy empowering me. I feel my soul's connection to the divine and God. The purpose of my life is revealed to me, and it is as glorious as all who are born on earth to woman and from man too. What a feeling of exhilaration—Spirit calls to me and moves me to become all that I am in this God moment. I am a little child but already so perceptive and aware of life and people. Why do we think and feel as we do? Is it that we are able to plug into the deepest part of our natures? When I share this with others, even strangers, I float off the ground in elation. There is no fear of being lost. I am both grounded and flying to Heaven at the same time. This has been and is reward enough for me.

EPILOGUE

NEW YORK TIMES writer, Nicholas D. Kristof, wrote an editorial February 4, 2016 that summarizes the need for my book. He referred to a recent documentary on "honor killings" that like slavery in the 19th Century, the foremost moral issue of the 21st Century that we must deal with is the worldwide abuse and oppression of so many women and girls. His final sentence was: "Chipping away at this pattern of gender injustice is in the interests of all of us. It is our century' great unfinished business." My thanks to you and all the men who support us. Our founding fathers asked God to ensure liberty and justice for all of us as long as we remain a good and moral nation.

1923—The LaRaia Family after immigrating to Torrington, CT. Anita's Dad is standing at the back, surrounded by his parents, and three of four brothers. His two sisters were not in the photo.

1928—Anita's Dad behind the counter
of his store in Torrington, CT.

1937—Portrait of Anita's Dad in tuxedo that
he signed to his outstanding daughter.

1944—Anita's Mother, Sylvia Cleopatra, at the back with her Family in Pennsylvania. In the photo are Anita's Field Marshall grandfather, grandmother, Aunt Rose and Uncle Emidio.

1945—Wedding photo of Anita's Mother and Father in his Navy uniform with her maternal Grandparents behind their house in Pennsylvania.

1949—Anita and her sister Diana in front of one of their Dad's cool cars—Graham, Packard, or Hudson.

1950—Anita as a three-year-old child wearing her Mother's wedding locket and the ruby and gold ring her Father gave her.

1960—The four LaRaia children, including big sister Anita, Diana, Laraine, and brother Lou celebrating his birthday.

1965—Anita's High School photo as co-Valedictorian.

1973—Anita in white bikini on the balcony of beach hotel in Greece. Photo taken by her London roommates. Anita lived and worked in London from 1971 to 1977.

1979—Knight's of Vine wine dinner with famous California winemaker Richard G. Peterson standing next to Anita in the center. Also in attendance Anita's best friend blonde Paulette and Dr. Kenneth Alonso, his wife Carmen, and parents.

1983—Anita on the deck of the home she shared with
her husband Michael in Atlanta when she worked
as the Georgia Sales Manager for Banfi Vintners.

1991—Anita on the set of wine video at the
time she won nationwide auditions.

1998--Kirlian Photography of Anita's large white and
gold Spiritual Aura, including her two purple spirit guides
visible below her ears. Everyone has electromagnetic
field. Anita's shows she has God-given wisdom as a
moral teacher that she worked hard to enhance.

Anita's dear departed husband Michael—
Her Jeweled Butterfly.

Back Cover Author Photo—1979—Anita at
wine tasting in home of the owners of the famous
Germany wine estate, JJ Prum, on the Mosel River.